GENERAL PRACTICE

as it was

GENERAL PRACTICE

as it was

A GP'S LIFE IN CANADA AND RURAL WALES

Dewi Rees MD FRCGP BS

For two outstanding GPs

Dr Harry Paddon MD DSc OC (of Labrador)
Dr Graham Davies OBE LRCP MRCS (of Wales)

First impression: 2012

Cover design: Y Lolfa
Cover photograph: John Copas
Labrador photographs: Isobel Watts
Other photographs: Anna Asquith and Eileen Rees

ISBN: 978 184771 412 1

FSC
Published and printed in Wales
on paper from well maintained forests
by Y Lolfa Cyf., Talybont, Ceredigion SY24 5HE
website www.ylolfa.com
e-mail ylolfa@ylolfa.com
tel 01970 832 304
fax 832 782

Contents

Introduction

THIS BOOK IS a biographical account of people, places and incidents. It is based on my own life but, where appropriate, it includes the experiences of general practitioners with whom I worked closely. To protect people's anonymity, a few names and places have been changed deliberately, some have been changed inadvertently because of memory lapses, but in most instances the correct names are given. In writing the book, I have been greatly helped by the advice of my daughter, Dr Eileen Rees, whose suggestions I have happily incorporated, and the helpful comments of my friend, Dr Sylvia Cree, a retired GP. The photographs of Labrador were taken by Isobel Watts whose father-in-law, Jack Watts, was a prominent member of the Labrador community in my time. Jack is mentioned in the book and I am grateful to Isobel for letting me have the photographs.

Dewi Rees
March 2012

1

Starting Work
in South Wales 1956–7

I BEGAN MY work as a doctor in August 1956. I was 27 years old and like most of my peers had served in the armed forces. When I qualified I had been married for three years and was the proud father of Eileen, a daughter only a few months old. As a student at St Thomas's Hospital, London I had received a grant from the Government to pay for my education, but my wife Valerie, a biochemist at the Hammersmith Hospital, was our main source of income during our early years together. We had met at a birthday party in London when we were both students, and were immediately drawn to each other. Asking her to marry me was the best, and wisest, thing I ever did and though I expected a long engagement, we were soon married and remained together for 54 years. She was the one true love of my heart and contributed to my life in so many different ways.

Newly-qualified doctors usually seek their first jobs at their own teaching hospital, and most of my friends did that. But I had the welfare of a young mother and baby to consider and did not want a post in London. Instead I applied for and obtained jobs in south Wales, so that Eileen and Valerie could live with Val's parents in Whitchurch, Cardiff, whilst I did my internships close by, initially at Bridgend General Hospital and then at the Caerphilly and District Miners' Hospital. These were not well-known hospitals but both provided me with a greater range of experience than I would have obtained at better-known centres. Bridgend Hospital was a particularly happy place but I felt a bit isolated at Caerphilly, as I was the only resident doctor in a hospital with 100 beds.

Bridgend General Hospital

Bridgend (in Welsh *Penybont-ar-Ogwr*) is situated just 22 miles to the west of Cardiff. The hospital was originally a workhouse and became part of the National Health Service (NHS) in 1948. The unit was closed in the 1990s and a new hospital established nearby. Of the five hospitals where I have worked in the UK, only the Llanidloes Cottage Hospital remains in use today. The rest have closed; some being replaced with new buildings, whilst services provided by the remainder have been relocated elsewhere. Similarly Bridgend, though a market town, was closely associated with the south Wales coal mining industry, but the collieries are no longer in use. However, the old hospital building still stands. It became a Grade II listed building in 1986 and is now used as a Community Health Clinic. The old Bridgend General Hospital had few resident staff – there were about ten of us all told. These included the surgical registrar (a Canadian), the obstetric registrar (from Sudan) and the senior casualty officer (a South African). It was a happy doctors' mess, disturbed only by the Suez crisis! We were all shocked by the event, not least because one of our members, as mentioned, was a Sudanese, for whom the crisis seemed very close to home.

Life as a junior hospital doctor was busy and fascinating – there was so much to experience and to learn. In common with my peers, I was overworked, but for the most part I was happy doing the job for which I had trained and was eager to practise. Our first year was spent in training posts which had to be completed before we could be fully registered as doctors with the General Medical Council. We were required to live in the hospital and were allowed out just one night a week and alternate weekends away, so I was unable to spend much time with my family. I was a house physician and worked on the medical ward, but as a junior doctor I was also required to man the Casualty Department on certain nights and weekends. I shall not forget my first weekend as the casualty officer. It was a Bank Holiday weekend Saturday and I was the only doctor there, and was dealing with minor casualties when a young woman was rushed into the unit on a stretcher. She had been brought from Ogmore-by-Sea, about 30 miles away, where she had got into difficulty swimming, and was pulled out of the water unconscious. Attempts to resuscitate her by the ambulance crew had not been successful and she was dead when she reached the hospital. An oxygen mask hung loosely from her face. On examining her I realised that it was futile to attempt to resuscitate her; cardiopulmonary resuscitation was not taught in those days, and sadly she had no chance of being revived after such a long journey in the ambulance. Her husband was standing close by and I had to tell him that she was dead. He looked at me in disbelief. Then the Casualty Sister quietly led him to her office, to provide the comfort and support that a man whose life had been so suddenly shattered needed. I had other casualties to care for, and gave them my attention.

A Surprising Encounter

Fifty years later I had a chance encounter in London with a nursing sister from Bridgend General Hospital. Although long retired I had been asked by the Royal College of General Practitioners to be its delegate at a conference in London on the medical care of prisoners. The subject interested me as I had worked as a counsellor at a Young Offenders' Institute and written about the high incidence of bereavement experienced by these teenagers. So I went to the conference and attended the morning session which I found excellent.

But I missed the afternoon session as I wanted to see Andrew Lloyd Webber's exhibition of Pre-Raphaelite Art at the Royal Academy in Piccadilly. Being in my late seventies I tended to tire easily and after walking around the galleries felt the need for a rest and a cup of coffee. I found my way to the coffee bar downstairs, purchased the coffee and sat down at the one vacant place available – at a refectory table which seated about twelve people and those present were mostly women. Eventually, the lady at the end of the table stood up and began to organise their departure. She spoke with a Welsh accent, so I turned to the lady sitting next to me and asked her where the group came from. "Oh we are from Bridgend," she said. "We have come to see the Lloyd Webber exhibition." In reply, I told her that I had had my first job at Bridgend Hospital, fifty years ago. "Oh, I used to work at the General," she said. "I was the sister on the medical ward." As we chatted, it became obvious that this lady had been the sister in charge of the ward when I had worked as a house physician at Bridgend. It was a fascinating encounter, an incident that Carl Jung would have labelled as indicative of *synchronicity*, "an acausal connecting principle acting within the psyche". In other words, a significant meeting that had no apparent cause.

The Caerphilly and District Miners' Hospital

Caerphilly (in Welsh *Caerffili*), a commuter town for Cardiff and Newport, is situated at the lower end of the Rhymney valley about 7 miles north of Cardiff. Its castle is the second largest in Britain (after Windsor Castle) and is one of the great medieval castles of Western Europe. It was built between 1268 and 1271 and is the first truly concentric castle to have been built in Britain. Apart from its size, it is also remarkable for the large-scale use of water as a defence. During the 1920s there were 29 pits in the Rhymney Valley and the Miners' Hospital was established in 1923 to provide health care for

24,000 miners and their families. The original building, called the Beeches, was a redbrick mansion that the miners' acquired from a mining engineer, Mr Fred Piggott. Each miner paid sixpence from their weekly wage of 12s.6d. for the purchase and construction of the hospital, the total cost being £30,000. The wards were named after local collieries. Perhaps the most significant name was Senghenydd, where an explosion in the mine on 14 October 1913 killed 439 men. It remains the worst mining accident to have occurred in the UK, and in terms of the loss of life, is one of the worst anywhere in the world.

I was fortunate to get the obstetric appointment at the Miners' Hospital. Obstetric jobs were highly prized in those days and each junior post had many applicants. The normal practice was for young doctors to spend their first year of training alternating between surgery and medicine, and then to specialise – the obstetric posts going to would-be general practitioners or those intending to be consultant obstetricians. At Bridgend, I was offered the obstetric post if I would do the surgical job first, but I declined the offer and was immensely fortunate to be given the post at the Miners' Hospital. In making my decision, the key factor was my age: I was 28 years old and needed to make rapid progress in my chosen field which was general practice.

I was the first doctor to be appointed a House Surgeon in obstetrics and gynaecology at the Miners' Hospital. At the time, obstetrics and gynaecology was an expanding department in the hospital, with a recently-appointed consultant and a part-time Senior Hospital Medical Officer (SHMO). Mine was the most junior of grades, but because there were no registrars or SHOs in post, my range of duties and responsibilities tended to be greater than if I had worked elsewhere. Consequently, I was allowed to undertake certain obstetric manoeuvres – the easier breech and forceps deliveries – which were normally performed by more experienced doctors. Luckily, I got on particularly well with the senior midwife, Sister Veale. We had no consultant anaesthetist attached to the unit. If an anaesthetic was required, it was given by a local GP. Because of my greater involvement, I regarded myself as a better obstetrician than I was, considering myself capable of doing just about everything except Caesarean sections. The moment of truth came when a local GP asked me if I would help with a home delivery. His patient had been in labour for some hours, was getting tired, and needed help in delivering the baby. He had decided that delivery by forceps was necessary and was looking for someone to give the anaesthetic. Would I help? I said that I could not give the anaesthetic but I could manage the forceps delivery. This was acceptable to him and he took me to the lady's house.

I have no clear recollection of the bedroom but it did contain a large bed with a soft mattress. The normal procedure was for the woman to lie on her left side, whilst the anaesthetic was being administered and the forceps applied. The anaesthetic, probably chloroform, would have been carefully dispensed, drop by drop, from a glass bottle on to a gauze pad that the anaesthetist held loosely over the patient's face. This initial procedure was managed easily and the doctor soon had the patient anaesthetised. Then I applied the forceps, again without any difficulty, but my attempt to deliver the baby was completely unsuccessful. Never mind how hard I pulled on the forceps the baby did not emerge. Eventually I had to tell the GP that I could not extract the child. He looked aghast, came to my side and seized hold of the forceps. Then he placed his left hand on the mother's buttocks, pushed firmly and just by pulling the forceps with his right hand extracted the baby with ease. The baby cried, its mother regained consciousness, the two were reunited and we were all happy. I then realised that I had failed because I had not applied counter pressure when pulling on the forceps. Instead of delivering the baby, I had just dragged the mother towards the edge of the bed. The deliveries in hospital had been simplified for me by Sister Veale – she always applied counter pressure during a forceps delivery, and I never noticed it. But then in hospital, forceps deliveries were always done with the mother in stirrups, not in the more dignified left lateral position.

Termination of Pregnancy

Two incidents at Caerphilly upset me. One involved a young married woman in her early twenties, who was referred by the Emergency Bed Service as an inevitable abortion. She was admitted at the weekend to the gynaecological ward and placed on the Monday morning operation list for uterine clearance. She was already in theatre when the ward sister came and informed the consultant that the patient had a low-grade temperature, so he decided to postpone the operation until Thursday. The patient was on antibiotics but she collapsed two days later, and when I phoned the consultant he told me to put her on anti-gas gangrene vaccine immediately, which I did. She died a dreadful death from gas gangrene of the womb.

The other incident involved a healthy woman in her later twenties with mitral stenosis. She was pregnant, in her second trimester, and was referred by a senior cardiologist for termination of a pregnancy that was threatening her life. I did the usual pre-op assessment, including a chest X-ray which looked normal and informed my consultant that she looked in good health and did not need to be terminated. Well so-and-so has referred her so we better go ahead he said, and she was listed for hysterotomy. In the theatre, there were just two of us standing alongside the anaesthetised patient. He said to me, it's time you did one, so we changed sides and I did the hysterotomy and terminated the pregnancy. I liked my consultant, but in retrospect felt unhappy with the process and after David Steel's Abortion Bill was passed by

Parliament, I never signed a green form. I knew my stance would not hinder terminations being performed, and always assured relevant patients that they would have no problems getting the foetus aborted. Later in 2004, my stance on this issue was severely criticised by a general practitioner whom I knew well. He argued that I had a duty to sign the forms in such cases, which I think is probably the prevalent position among GPs today. If so, I would not want to be a modern GP, and in any case would probably have difficulty in finding a practice that would accept me as a partner.

My First Tractor Accident

My first excursion as a doctor outside the hospital came whilst I was working at the Miners' Hospital. I happened to be in the Casualty Department, which local GPs manned in those days, when a police car stopped outside and two policemen came into the unit. They were looking for a doctor who would accompany them to a tractor accident and help with the casualty. Being keen and inexperienced I volunteered to go. So, we got into their car and drove to a nearby hillside where an overturned tractor was resting on its side. The tractor had no safety cab and the driver's dead body lay close by. Birds were already pecking at the brains that had escaped from his fractured skull. It was obvious that my presence had been requested merely to confirm the fact of death, so that his body could be removed and a coroner's inquest begun. I had been given no indication by the police that they knew the man was dead, nor did I learn anything else about him or of the family that had been bereaved so tragically. This was a one-off encounter. There was no follow-up, or any expectation that anything similar might occur again. Yet, eight years later, when I had joined a practice in rural Wales, I worked in an area where agricultural tractor accidents were frequent and wrote the first account of such accidents to appear in the British medical press.

Bargoed: Introduction to General Practice

My ventures outside the Miners' Hospital to a tractor accident and domiciliary midwifery were just preliminary encounters with the kind of family medicine that I was to practice later. But my first real experience of general practice became possible only in August 1957, when I had completed my statutory 12 months hospital internship, and became eligible for full registration with the General Medical Council. I was looking for a trainee post in general practice, when a GP in Bargoed asked me to do a week's locum so that he could take his wife and children on holiday. This I agreed to do, wanting the experience. Together with Valerie and baby Eileen, I moved into the doctor's terraced house in Bargoed, a Welsh mining village. By modern standards it was a small house for a doctor, but posts were difficult to get in general practice in the 1950s, and people adjusted as best they could. My employer was an independent man who did not mingle easily. When his fellow GPs established a group practice and invited him to join them, he chose to remain as a single-handed practitioner, though he did agree to use the same purpose-built surgery as the other practitioners. This was good for me as I was not completely isolated and the other doctors were available to help and advise me, and were willing to do so.

One occasion does stand out. It occurred when a burly miner walked into the surgery complaining of abdominal pain. His pain was located in the right lower quadrant of the abdomen, and the area was tender to touch. I could not believe the reality of the diagnosis that confronted me. The man had walked into the surgery with acute appendicitis and in my limited experience people didn't do that. They were brought into hospital on a stretcher by ambulance. Luckily I had the good sense to ask one of the GPs to examine him and to accept the advice he gave. He agreed with the diagnosis and told me to send the man into hospital.

He went to the Caerphilly and District Miners' Hospital where he came under the care of Mr Jenkins, a surgeon whom I knew quite well. Known affectionately as "Spot Jenkins" he had been a great help to me one Bank Holiday, when I was alone in the hospital and had to deal with an emergency that I had not encountered before. On that occasion, a woman was admitted to the Miners' Hospital in an advanced stage of pregnancy and with abdominal pain. She was not in labour but the pain was severe and suggestive of blood in the peritoneum. My consultant was away and I phoned Spot for advice. Though not an obstetrician, he came from Cardiff to see the patient, confirmed my provisional diagnosis (a ruptured uterus) and arranged her admission to an obstetric unit in Cardiff, where her baby was delivered by Caesarean section. Both mother and baby did well. Spot was an easy person to get on with and we sometimes lunched together when he was at the hospital. Sadly, I learnt some years later that he had committed suicide while on holiday alone in Malta. I couldn't believe it. Such sad moments are an inherent part of medical practice and the suicide rate among doctors tends to be particularly high.

2
Eltham, London 1957–8

A GP trainee post in Eltham

THE YEARS THAT followed World War II were accompanied by vast changes in social and political structures throughout the world. The medical services were also affected in many countries, and this was particularly evident in the United Kingdom where Clement Atlee's newly elected Labour Government established the National Health Service (NHS) in 1948. The idea was revolutionary. Its purpose was to replace private medicine with a system of state-funded health care for all citizens from conception to the grave. The British Medical Association opposed the idea at first, but eventually agreed to co-operate, and the NHS soon became established as an integral part of the British social system. The Labour Government also extended people's access to universities. This it did in two ways. Firstly by paying students' tutorial fees to the universities. Secondly, by contributing towards students' living expenses, the proportion given being determined by the family's income. The availability of these grants was crucial in enabling many people to receive the further education that they obtained. My elder brother, Hywel, was the first member of my family to go to university. I tended to follow his lead, and his choice of medicine and general practice almost certainly influenced my decision to pursue those paths.

On completion of my hospital appointments, I was entitled to be fully registered with the General Medical Council (GMC), a necessary prerequisite to working in general practice. That achieved, I immediately sought a placement as a trainee GP, a newly-created post within the NHS. Its establishment had been recommended by the Spens Committee (on the remuneration of general practitioners) in 1946, as a way of providing vocational training for future general practitioners. Although not among the first trainees, I was probably one of the earliest people to join the scheme. It eased me into general practice and provided a better salary than that received as a hospital doctor. The hours we worked were also less onerous. The trainers benefited too. They obtained the assistance of a qualified doctor without cost to themselves, and also a useful addition to their income.

I applied for two trainee posts, both offering accommodation for my family. One was in Grimsby, the other in south London. I accepted the first post I was offered, it was with Dr W H Myers, who practised alone from his home in Eltham, south London. His surgery was slightly avante garde for those days, possessing a small but separate examination room. With the job, I was offered the opportunity to rent a furnished flat in nearby Blackheath. I accepted both offers, bought a car and moved my family into this new accommodation. Eileen was about 18 months at the time, and practised her walking and climbing skills on the fire escape that linked our fourth floor flat to the garden below. The ground floor flat had been converted into a dentist's surgery, with a sun lounge and aviary facing the garden. The birds were lovely and a source of constant delight. It may be coincidental, but when Eileen completed her studies at Leicester University her first job was with Sir Peter Scott, the eminent naturalist and painter, to take forward the study of Bewick's swans at the Wildfowl and Wetlands Trust, Slimbridge, Gloucestershire. She is now well known as an ornithologist and is author of the standard work on the Bewick's swan.

Eltham has changed a great deal since September 1957, probably more than most other regions in the United

Kingdom. Then it was a white working-class area where Herbert Morrison, Home Secretary in Churchill's wartime government, and Deputy Prime Minister in Attlee's government, had his home. Now, fifty years later, Eltham is one of the most ethnically diverse areas of the United Kingdom with 12.3 per cent of its population having been born outside the UK. This diversity of cultures and nationalities has helped to transform the area and perhaps the work undertaken by its general practitioners, though the facilities for dealing with patients, has changed also. Dr Myers, like most city GPs, had no receptionist, no practice manager, no practice nurse, no partners nor any other aids. At the time he differed from most London GPs in one major respect only. He had a trainee assistant, the others did not. I was his second trainee.

In 1957, a GP's income depended mainly on the number of people who were registered with him or her as NHS patients. The more patients, the better the income. A patient's age and the location of the practice could also affect the income. Older patients had an increased weighting that brought in more money, whilst doctors working in rural areas received an additional mileage allowance, determined by the distance a patient's home was situated from the surgery. Dispensing practices were also paid a 'dispensing fee' similar to that paid to pharmacists. It followed that the remuneration received by a dispensing doctor in a rural practice could differ considerably from that paid to an inner-city GP. The latter often bolstered their income by accepting large numbers of patients, 3,000 or more, and many did so, probably to the detriment of good practice. In contrast, the rural doctor had fewer patients but could afford to spend more time with each patient and still have a good income. I remember being told as a student that the standard of general practice improved the further a GP was located from a teaching hospital. I think that assessment was true then, but may no longer be applicable.

21

In 1957, General Practitioners could increase their income in other ways if they wished. Many had part-time appointments in hospitals, industry, commerce, in schools and infant welfare clinics. Providing anaesthesia at dental clinics was also quite lucrative, and work of this type, was undertaken by Dr Myers and myself. He had very few, if any, private patients though occasionally visitors from abroad offered to pay a fee when they consulted me, I never accepted any such payment nor to my knowledge did my principal. That may seem strange now, but we were proud of the NHS and of the underlying concept that patients did not pay directly for the treatment they received. Later, when I joined a practice in rural Wales, I found that my partners also had no private patients. Everyone was expected to enrol as an NHS patient, even the very rich.

Dr W H Myers – my trainer

My trainer's practice surgery was located in his home, as was common at that time. My family doctor in south Wales had also practised from his own home and I remember seeing him only twice as a child: on both occasions he visited me at home and sent me into the fever hospital, the first time with scarlet fever, the second time with diphtheria. I saw Dr Myers' wife infrequently and their only child rarely. She had contracted poliomyelitis in childhood and wore a calliper, having been struck by the disease before vaccines became available to mitigate its effect. The Myers' were amateur ballroom dancers of international repute and were particularly successful competitively in the Latin-American dances. He enjoyed cultivating orchids, his other interests being anaesthetics and the Territorial Army. Dr Myers had served as a medical officer during the war and retained the rank of major in the TA. He may have acquired his skill in anaesthesia whilst serving in the army, and it was a skill he enjoyed practising in civilian life, having an appointment as an anaesthetist at the Eltham and Mottingham Cottage Hospital, and regular sessions at local dental clinics. The Eltham and Mottingham Hospital was a rarity in Greater London in 1957 as, following the establishment of the NHS, it was the only cottage hospital still to provide GPs with access to their own beds, the others having been closed or converted to other uses. The closure of cottage hospitals was a great blow to many communities throughout the country and, in my opinion, was one reason for the enthusiastic support given to the Hospice movement once Cicely Saunders had opened St Christopher's Hospice in 1968. The new hospices provided a terminal care facility that once was a function of the cottage hospitals, and both attracted local support. Of course, much has changed in Eltham since 1957. A new children's hospice, the Demelze Hospice, was opened in the town centre in June 2009, and the cottage hospital is now closed. I enjoyed caring for my own patients in the cottage hospital and it was one reason for my choosing to go to Eltham. It was a facility available to me for most of my time as a GP.

Dr Myers taught me the basic skills of dental anaesthesia and I had regular sessions as a dental anaesthetist. It was a role that I never enjoyed – we anaesthetised patients whilst they were seated in dental chairs, and I found it a bit scary. Nitrous oxide and trilene were administered routinely, but we also used intravenous barbiturates. I was not a competent anaesthetist but luckily there were no disasters and all the patients regained consciousness. Dr Myers also introduced me to the administrative aspects of general practice, mainly to the various official forms we used and issued. People needed medical certificates more frequently than now, and would come for a certificate just to declare themselves fit or unfit for work. These consultations often required no more than a minute or two. Other forms enabled us to request a wide range of tests, at the Radiology and Pathology Departments of the Brooke General Hospital (now closed) on nearby Shooters Hill. Older GPs arranged relatively few tests but I requested all the tests that I would have undertaken as a hospital doctor. The service was excellent. Providing general practitioners with access to such tests was innovative in the 1950s, and crucial for the development of general practice into its present structure. Equally innovative at the time was the decision by the Brooke General Hospital to provide GPs with a sterile syringe service, which enabled us to collect the blood to be tested. The syringes were made of glass and could be reused once sterilised. Plastic syringes became available only later. With this excellent support from the local hospital, I was able to undertake most of the diagnostic tests that I had used on hospital wards.

Working alone

Six weeks after I joined his practice Dr Myers became ill with acute hepatitis. He was unable to work and I found myself doing all the surgeries, home visits and night calls alone. Fortunately he did have an arrangement with neighbouring practices, which enabled those in the scheme to have some nights and weekends off. But whilst he was ill I did his stint, and was on call for the other practices in the scheme for two nights a week and two weekends in five. Even when he was ill this provided me with more free time than I had enjoyed as a hospital doctor, and during our year at Eltham we would take Eileen to some of her favourite places. She liked to go to Greenwich Park to see the deer and play on the swings, and to London Zoo where she loved all the animals and birds – except the lions, which scared her too much. In the Lions' House she would hide her face in a checked comfort blanket which, aged one to two years, she took everywhere. Yet, as I think back, she never refused to go into the Lion's House despite her fear of the lions.

I had no problems managing the practice whilst Dr Myers

was away. This involved a morning and evening surgery each weekday, and probably just one on Saturday. Patients would queue in the waiting room and most were in and out very quickly, sometimes within a minute or two. Many would require just a certificate to say that they were fit or unfit for work. If someone needed more attention, there was no problem about providing it, whether this was a physical examination or just time to listen to their problems. Listening was an important part of the consultation, it was my main therapeutic tool for people who were depressed or anxious. I cannot remember referring anyone to a psychiatrist and most of the psychotropic drugs that are prescribed now were not available in the 1950s. Barbiturates were the main sedatives and largactil (chlorpromazine) the only tranquilliser. Antidepressant drugs had not been invented then. Looking back, this lack of psychotropic drugs may not have been a bad thing; the range of choice is almost too great now, and other options such as Cognitive Therapy are also available. On the other hand, when the first antidepressant drugs (imipramine and phenelzine) became available in 1959, I was working in a psychiatric unit and the availability of those frontline drugs to general practitioners was an important reason for my returning to general practice and not pursuing a career in psychiatry.

The Eltham practice didn't provide midwifery services. Pregnant patients were referred to the local midwife or obstetric unit for care and delivery. This simplified our workload but I did deal with two miscarriages. One was a spontaneous abortion in a young woman, pregnant for the first time. I knew she was thrilled with the pregnancy and when she lost the baby we were both upset, though of course medics try to hide this from their patients. The other case was different. It involved a woman in her late twenties who I believe was a call girl, and had had the pregnancy terminated when this was an illegal act. She was an attractive person both physically and as an individual, and lived in a detached

25

house with her mother, another pleasant person, but I didn't care for the man who patrolled the house when I visited. He was not the husband or partner and had 'pimp' written all over him. My patient was losing a ten- to fourteen-week-old foetus and refused to go into hospital, though I tried to persuade her to do so. Luckily the miscarriage passed off uneventfully; she came to see me once afterwards, for a health check, and everything appeared normal. Two other things I remember about her: she said that her father died when she was young and that she worked as a book-keeper, though I think that the latter was a cover for her role as a high-class prostitute. Certainly, the house seemed too upmarket for an unmarried book-keeper.

Hospital admissions

Arranging a patient's admission to hospital was easy in London. It was done through the Emergency Bed Service (EBS). If a patient needed to be admitted to hospital urgently, the GP phoned the Bed Service and the EBS found a bed for the individual in a London hospital. On one occasion I was asked to visit a man with asthma. He was a Welshman who had some difficulty in breathing. His chest was a bit tight, I wasn't particularly worried and might have treated him at home, but thought it was safer to admit him to hospital. So I EBS'd him. Within an hour, there was a telephone call from the Eltham and Mottingham Cottage Hospital to inform me that my patient had arrived and needed to be seen. I wasn't sure what they meant, as I had not arranged to admit anyone to the cottage hospital and did not expect it to be involved with the Emergency Bed Service, but I went as summoned and found the man in a dreadful state. He was breathless and cyanotic; I wasn't sure how best to manage him as he was so ill, so I phoned a consultant physician who attended immediately and told me what to do. It is so long ago that I can't remember his precise advice, but it was probably to start treatment with steroids which were not widely used then. Anyway, the outcome was good and the man made a complete recovery, though I still remember my fright on seeing him in hospital.

In the 1950s, a domiciliary visit by a consultant physician or surgeon was an important feature of general practice. A consultant would always visit when asked, and the GP would always meet the consultant in the patient's home. It was a learning experience for both and many problems could be resolved by these joint visits. I remember one occasion when the outcome was a little surprising. I went to see a woman with abdominal pain and being unsure of the diagnosis asked a senior consultant for his advice. We met in the patient's house, and he agreed that the most likely diagnosis was acute appendicitis, and advised me to EBS the patient. Some hours later, I phoned the hospital to see how the woman had progressed and was told she was alright and had needed no specific treatment. Perhaps sensing that the hospital doctor regarded the admission as inappropriate, I pointed out that the patient had been seen by a senior surgeon and had been admitted on his advice. The registrar dashed off immediately to examine her again, then came back to inform me that she was alright. That incident taught me that assessing a patient in hospital could be remarkably different from doing so at home. This is even truer now than then, as the range of equipment/tests available in hospitals today far exceeds those that were available fifty years ago.

Home visits

Home visits were always an important aspect of general practice in the past but are undertaken much less frequently today. Our contract required us to be on call for 24 hours a day, 7 days a week, but that no longer applies. This personal responsibility to a registered patient applied even when another doctor (a partner for instance) covered the practice in one's absence, as any breach of contract was the responsibility of the GP with whom the patient was registered.

The pattern of illness has changed too. Preventative medicine has greatly reduced the incidence of infectious diseases such as measles, poliomyelitis, influenza and lobar pneumonia, and a clean air policy has eliminated the smog that once engulfed our major towns and cities and made breathing difficult for many. Paramedics did not exist in those days and were not available to visit patients with life-threatening diseases; they were seen by their GP. Domiciliary visits were a normal feature of a GP's life and when I visited a child in Eltham I would always look carefully at the mother, and check her for anaemia. If she seemed anaemic, and many were in those days, I would send a blood sample to the Brooke Hospital and, if the presumptive diagnosis of iron deficiency anaemia was confirmed, I would treat it appropriately. It was such a simple thing to do but effective. I remember visiting a woman who had been investigated for amoebiasis at the London Hospital for Tropical Diseases. The results were negative, but because she had lived abroad and was not well, I sent her directly to the Pathology laboratory at the Brooke Hospital where a sample of her faeces was examined, and the suspected diagnosis was confirmed and treated. She was the first of only four patients with a tropical disease that I encountered as a medical practitioner, the others having contracted malaria, leprosy, and meningococcal meningitis whilst abroad. The patient with amoebiasis also had an iron deficiency anaemia which needed supplementary iron. Compared with the past, iron deficiency anaemia is a relatively uncommon condition in women in the UK today, probably because the contraceptive pill reduces menstrual loss and diets are much better. But it was a lovely condition to treat, as the patient became visibly stronger within a few weeks of receiving iron supplements. Also her children's health was likely to improve as she was better able to care for them.

Kidbrooke School

Kidbrooke School was the first comprehensive school to be purpose-built in Britain. It was opened in 1954 in our practice area, and was an enormous addition to the locality. It was an innovative school with over a thousand pupils, but at that time it was too big to provide a sense of community to the staff or children. I worked there on a sessional basis, seeing children in clinics for the local authority, and gained some insight into its early teething problems. In 2005 it was re-designated as a single Specialist Arts College and though still large, now specialises in Media, Drama and Art. Since it was opened, other forms of comprehensive education have been evolved, and governments are learning to provide them with more cohesive social and academic structures than was possible during the experimental phase that Kidbrooke School inaugurated. Although my involvement was brief, I remain interested, having been one of the first doctors to work at the school and know that considerable changes have been made since then. A possible catalyst was the killing of a 14-year-old boy, C J Rickard, as he left Kidbrooke School for home in January 1997. He was attacked and killed with a macheté by a gang from the nearby Thomas Tallis School. This gang likened themselves to the Chinese Triads and called themselves the Golden Snakes. His killer was only 15 years old.

Since the death of C J Rickard, important changes have been made at Kidbrooke School, most notably the establishment of a drop-in health centre called Teentalk@Kidbrooke, which is based on the school's premises. Teentalk@Kidbrooke is the first of its kind in the London area. It is a 'teacher free zone' led by a multidisciplinary staff in partnership with a wide range

29

of specialist services with its own co-ordinator. It offers confidential counselling for students who may be unlikely to seek support in more formal health centres. It runs regular clinics and provides a varied range of activities at lunchtime and after school, including sport, art, technology and homework support. The drop-in centre is open daily and there are extensive activities for involving parents, including drug awareness talks. Its impact on the pupils is considerable, with 900 recorded visits per term and a dramatic reduction in birth rates for those girls still at school. On leaving Eltham in 1958, I never imagined that Kidbrooke School would be so closely involved in health and social care, but wonder to what extent the local GPs are currently involved. At the end of my contract, I left Eltham to work as a locum with Dr Logan of Whittlesey.

Dr Logan of Whittlesey

Having finished my time at Eltham I should have taken a holiday, but instead I did a week's locum at Whittlesey, near Peterborough, with a partnership that had two doctors and a receptionist. Dr Dan Logan was the senior doctor, the practice surgery being located in his house, the Chestnuts. There was just one memorable patient, an elderly lady who lived alone in a house, where a sense of gloom pervaded the whole building permanently. She looked so dejected and miserable, and the reason was obvious, her right arm was gangrenous from the elbow to the fingertips. It was not a new development but had been present for weeks. Amputation was the obvious remedy but she refused to be seen by a surgeon, or treated surgically. She just lay and gazed at her dead arm. I am not sure why I was sent to see her, it was probably a routine visit to a disabled woman who could not be totally neglected. There was nothing I could do, but the memory of that transient meeting remains with me still.

At Whittlesey, the receptionist told me that Dr Logan had been awarded the George Medal, but that he never spoke about it. So I never enquired about it until recently, when I contacted Carol Woods at the Jenner Health Centre in Whittlesey. Carol had joined the centre when Dr Logan opened it in December 1969. She worked with him for many years and says that he was a very well liked and respected character in the town. He died on 27 November 2000, and his stepson, Patrick St Leger, mentioned the George Medal at the memorial service. Patrick said that Dr Logan, and a colleague, were both awarded the medal for their heroism when a hospital in London was bombed and an incendiary device discovered. He also said that the men 'put the bomb in a tin bath and took it outside', because *matron* had told them to do so. "Get that thing out of here!" she commanded and Dr Logan always claimed it was taken out because he was scared of matron!

I found a fuller account of the incident in the supplement of the *London Gazette*, 14 March 1941. It reports the award of a George Medal to Dr D C Logan, assistant medical officer of health and resident medical officer, and to Dr M Kahill house surgeon, both of Clayponds Emergency Hospital, London. It states:

> A time bomb penetrated the roof of the diphtheria block at the Clayponds Hospital coming to rest among the debris on the floor of the bathroom without exploding. Dr Logan and Dr Kamill, who had experienced the results of previous bombings on the hospital, arranged for the evacuation of the patients. They carried out their duties with coolness and courage, regardless of any danger to themselves, and prevented the possibility of great damage being done to the hospital buildings and to the houses of people adjoining. There is no doubt that by their initiative and devotion to duty Drs Logan and Kamill saved many lives.

Carol Woods shared other recollections of Dr Logan with me, and related two stories that were typical of Dr Logan. She said:

Every evening Dr Logan would leave the surgery with the words "Goodnight Miss Preston – thank you for today and I leave Dr Watson in sole charge." This was his ritual for as long as I can remember. You always treated Dr Logan with the greatest respect. However, one evening, out he came from his consulting room and said "Goodnight Miss Preston – thank you for today – has Dr Watson gone?" "Yes, Dr Logan" I said "And he left you in sole charge"! That is the only time I ever saw him laugh so much he had to use his white handkerchief to wipe his tears!

Carol Woods also told me that Dr Logan worked at a surgery at RAF Upwood once a week. "One day," she said, "he locked his keys in his car. He phoned the surgery to say send Miss Preston to the rescue (me being the only one with a car, aged 20, albeit a £30 Mini named Blue!). I had to go to Mrs Logan and pick up his keys and drive to RAF Upwood. On arrival I was escorted, giving me the most profound impression of importance, to Dr Logan's surgery. There I was greeted and thanked profusely by Dr Logan who then told me to go straight to Jubilee Garage (wow – he is going to fill my Blue with petrol) where Mr Trayford would put in one gallon. I thanked him very much, stopping short of giving a curtsey and walking out backwards!"

Dr John Hunt 1905–87

To write of 'General Practice as it was' and not mention John Hunt would be an enormous error. John Hunt was a physician who straddled the pre- and post- World War II years. In the 1930s, he was recognised as a physician of exceptional ability and potential eminence, but after World War II he chose to be a GP when that role carried little status and was not sought after by ambitious men. During the war he worked as a neurological specialist in the Royal Air Force with the rank of wing commander, but he did not enjoy it much and in 1945 he set up an independent practice in central London. This was an unusual practice, with its own X-ray service and pathology laboratory, facilities that many GPs did not obtain until much later. I met him only briefly when he was simply Dr John Hunt, not yet knighted or made a peer of the realm. His main contribution to family medicine was probably his central role in helping to establish the Royal College of General Practitioners, and later in helping to establish similar colleges in Commonwealth countries.

One aspect of John Hunt's life, which caught my attention, was his interest in religion. He was not a regular churchgoer, and not an ardent Christian, but he was interested in religion and wrote and talked about it. His first 'clinical paper' was on the 'fakirs' of Hyderabad, and another paper was 'Religion and the Family Doctor'. His practice was eclectic. He never joined the NHS and only had private patients who tended to be scattered across London and its neighbouring areas. They included Sir Alexander Fleming, the Sackville family and Sir Thomas Beecham. When visiting his patients, which included visits to centres such as the London Clinic and the King Edward VII Hospital for Officers, he would travel in cars usually driven by lady chauffeurs, partly because his vision was poor but also because he used the time to record his meticulous notes.[1] Sometimes I wonder if he was a general practitioner in the real sense of the term. I think it is unlikely, as he did little obstetrics or trauma care, and was essentially a general physician with an elite and scattered clientele.

3

Labrador, Newfoundland 1958–9

IN THE 1950s, the only training posts designed specifically for general practice were of the type that I had just completed with Dr Myers. General practice was not regarded as a specialty then, and when in 1972 I submitted my thesis for the London MD it could not be registered within that discipline. Instead, it was registered and awarded as a contribution to psychiatry. After Eltham, I needed another job and sought one that would help to prepare me for my future in general practice. I was keen to get experience of tropical medicine, and to work in Africa or Asia, but Valerie refused to countenance such a move, being fearful for Eileen. We reached a compromise when I saw an advertisement for a post as Assistant Medical Officer with the International Grenfell Association (IGA) in Labrador, a charitable organisation that provided a medical service to the people of north-east Canada. A newly-built house was part of the package; the contract was for two years, with the IGA paying all our passages, or just one year if I paid our fares back to the UK. I chose the latter option. I was to be based at North West River where a modern hospital, staffed by two English nurses, had been constructed a few years earlier. My role was to help Dr Tony Paddon, a local man, to provide a medical service for the ethnically diverse people (Eskimos, American Indians and settlers) who lived in Central Labrador and the villages along the Labrador coast. Val and I were interviewed for the post in Central London by a member of the Bowater Company, a firm with extensive interests in Canada, and we were accepted. Whoever made our travel arrangements expedited them quickly, as soon we were flying from Gatwick to Gander, with Eileen sleeping peacefully throughout the trip. The Gander we reached was a very basic airport, with a noisy hostel and bunks instead of beds, but it was good to reach it safely and begin the next stage of the journey to St Anthony in the north of Newfoundland.

Dr Tony Paddon MD DSc OC (1914-2000)

Tony Paddon met us at St Anthony's Hospital, then the focal point of the IGA's medical services in north-east Canada. This initial meeting was brief, and I have little recollection of it, but I have a clear memory of an incident that followed soon afterwards in the town's harbour. We were to travel north on a boat named the Maraval, and the crew was untying the ship from the bollards on the harbour wall, when a hawser flew loose and knocked one of the men overboard. We all rushed to the edge of the boat to see how he was coping but not Tony Paddon. He ran to the ship's side, jumped overboard and joined the man in the water. Both were pulled out unhurt and went below to dry and change but, thinking back, Tony's leap was the response that the people of Labrador expected of their doctors. Sir Wilfred Grenfell, the founder of the IGA, was a remarkably brave and adventurous man who recorded his various exploits in his widely-read books. He set the pattern and Tony's father, Dr Harry Paddon, also showed great courage and endurance during his years on the coast. Many years later my partner, Dr Graham Davies, reacted in a similar way in mid Wales. When summoned to help a drowning man, he arrived at the Van Pool to find the ambulance crew and various bystanders gazing hesitantly into the dark water. Graham, then in his seventies, called for a rope, tied it around his waist and plunged immediately

35

into the treacherous water. His attempt to save a life was not successful, but his selfless act was typical of the man.

William Anthony Paddon was born in Indian Harbour, Labrador in July 1914. He was the son of an English doctor and an American nurse and, like his parents, dedicated his life to the people of Labrador. He was multi-talented, the sort of general medical practitioner that it would be difficult to meet again, and his important contributions to the life of people in Labrador have been recognised in various ways. The Memorial University of Newfoundland awarded him an honorary DSc, he was appointed a member of the Order of Canada (raised to officer in 1988) and, most significantly, was the first Labradorean to be appointed Lieutenant Governor of Newfoundland. Tony was a magistrate for many years, and his stories of life in that capacity included an occasion when he sentenced a man for beating his wife. The couple lived in a cabin among the trees and, as a punishment, the man was required to cut and deliver sufficient timber to the local school to keep it warm during the winter. It was some months before Dr Paddon met the wife again, and he was surprised at her bitterness towards him. He had not realised that, once they returned home, the husband would make her carry out the sentence, and be the person who cut and delivered the wood to the school.

Tony went to school in the USA. He trained as a doctor at the New York Medical School, and obtained his MD in 1940. After completing his internships, he returned to Canada and volunteered to join the armed forces, expecting to join the Air Force as he had a pilot's licence, but that hope was soon dashed. When the recruiting officer learnt that he was a doctor, he was told that he could not be a combatant and would have to serve as a medic. So Dr Paddon joined the Royal Canadian Navy as a surgeon, reaching the rank of Lieutenant Commander and serving on a destroyer off the coast of Normandy on D-day.

After demobilisation, he returned to North West River to continue the socio-medical work his father had started, and his mother had maintained following her husband's early death. He played a central role in the life of Labrador throughout the remainder of the twentieth century and helped to introduce many of the changes – social and medical – that were needed in a region where there were three ethnic groups, much poverty, and where the winter temperature, which usually ranged from –10°C to –15°C, could fall suddenly to –30°C. The summer months were brief and could be made surprisingly unpleasant by the large numbers of troublesome insects, most memorably mosquitoes and black flies that inhabited the area.

Whilst seeking to advance needed changes, Tony's and the government's plans did not always reflect the wishes of the indigenous peoples, the Inuit (Eskimo) and Innu (Indian). This was most evident in my time with the closing of Hebron, then the most northern Inuit village in Labrador. The people wished to remain in their huts but were forced to leave by the closure of essential facilities, such as the Hudson Bay store. Their views were not even canvassed before the decision was finalised in 1959. The reason for this omission was simple; the Inuit were not considered to be responsible citizens with rights equal to those of the European settlers. Instead they were regarded as grown up children, an attitude initiated by the early Christian missionaries who came to Labrador in the eighteenth century. One point of discrimination was that the sale of alcohol to the Inuit was forbidden by law. Consequently, they brewed their own beer, which occasionally resulted in a death from botulism. A suspected case of botulism was admitted to North West River hospital whilst I was there, but the diagnosis was not confirmed and the individual survived.

Dr Harry Paddon LRCP MRCS (1881–1940)

Tony's father, Dr Henry Locke Paddon, came to Labrador in 1912 at the request of the Royal National Missions to Deep Sea Fishermen (RNMDSF) who had employed him on ships in the North Sea. Known to the locals as the Land of Cain, Labrador was a beautiful but desolate country with a population of only about 4,000 people, yet it suited Harry Paddon. From early childhood he had wanted to be a missionary, but not an evangelist. He wanted to be a practical helper – a healer rather than a preacher. He was a sportsman, not an academic. He liked the outdoor life and did not want to be enclosed indoors. He decided to train as a doctor later in life than most men, and was 31 years old when he passed his final medical examination in 1911 at St Thomas's Hospital, London.

Having qualified with the conjoint diploma, he worked for a short time in a Birmingham hospital, then as a surgeon with the fishing fleets in the North Sea under the aegis of RNMDSF. The men on those boats did hard and dangerous work, and the surgeons accompanying them were often required to amputate digits and limbs, and suture gaping wounds. It was a life that suited Harry Paddon. In Labrador, he established a base at Indian Harbour, close to where the Newfoundland fleets fished off the Labrador coast for cod. When the fishing season was over and the ships returned home, he moved inland to central Labrador and established his first hospital on the north bank of Lake Melville at a place called North West River. In 1912 he met Mina Gilchrist, an American nurse and they were married the following year.

She was still resident in North West River when I arrived there. Tony, the first of their four sons, was born at Indian Harbour in 1914. Harry and Mina were in England at the outbreak of World War I and he considered volunteering for the armed forces, but he abandoned the idea and spent the war years as the only doctor in Labrador, a region where he had to deal with much poverty, malnutrition, and a near epidemic of tuberculosis.

TB remained a major problem in Labrador until anti-tuberculosis drugs and effective surgical interventions became available. At North West River I saw many people who had thoracoplasty scars after surgery at St Anthony's Hospital and we continued to treat many others with streptomycin, isoniazid (INH) and para-aminosalicylic acid (PAS). Fortunately, the struggle against TB was almost over then and there were no new cases of active tuberculosis. BCG vaccination was never used in Labrador as it was considered to be unhelpful, which I found interesting as I was immunised with the BCG vaccine whilst a medical student at St Thomas's. It is still given to teenagers in developed countries and to infants elsewhere, but routine use of BCG in Caucasian children, who are not otherwise at risk, is now considered questionable.

Harry Paddon was confronted by many problems that I never met. Before he died he wrote in his diary: "Twenty-five years ago, the lack of knowledge of hygiene alone was enough to maintain an almost epidemic of TB. The deficient ventilation, the common water dipper passed hand-to-hand and mouth-to-mouth, as well as other eating and drinking utensils recklessly shared by diseased and healthy alike – all these were enabling tuberculosis to reap a ghastly toll."[2] Nutritional disease was another problem that he worked hard to eliminate. Scurvy, beriberi and rickets were common in Labrador when he arrived in 1912, mainly because the cause of those diseases had not been fully determined or generally accepted. The textbook of medicine that he took to Labrador said of beriberi, "It has been attributed to unsuitable food, but the cause is not yet really known."[3] Harry was a general practitioner par excellence, with many roles within the community he served. In a summary of his life's work he said: "Having tried to combine the roles of small institutional physician and surgeon, family doctor and friend, parish priest, amateur navigator and pilot, justice of the peace, promoter of education and agriculture, and finally, financial campaigner, I can only frankly admit that the task had been beyond me. Nonetheless, there has been a good deal of interest, humour and adventure in trying."[4]

There was also great grief. As soldiers began to drift back from the European war, Spanish Flu was spreading worldwide and eventually reached the people of Labrador. The first returning Labradorean volunteers were put ashore 300 miles from home, and had to walk across the frozen ice on snowshoes to reach their families. But the flu preceded their return home; a ship's crew with cargo for North West River had already brought Spanish flu to the settlement. There were about 100 people in the community; most succumbed but only two died which, in retrospect, was a remarkably small number. Elsewhere its effect was more devastating. The sickness arrived without warning, bringing a strain of influenza that was so lethal that victims could die in hours. The illness began with a high fever, pains in the limbs and back, coughs and rigors. Breathing became difficult with people bleeding into their own lungs. Approximately one third of the Inuit population of Labrador died during the epidemic.

When reports of these deaths first reached Dr Paddon at North West River they seemed unbelievable. On the coast at Cartwright, one quarter of the population had died and over seventy orphaned children were being cared for by relatives, many of them bereaved. Further north at Okak with its population of 270, every man had been wiped out and only thirty-nine women and children had survived. At Hebron, with a population of 170, every man died. Hunger followed quickly with two important sources of food, grouse and rabbits, having been slaughtered by hordes of foxes. But everyone did their best to help, and for Dr Paddon this meant visiting the devastated communities by dog team.

When he reached North River (not North West River) he found that eleven corpses had been collected from its four houses and placed in a common grave. In one house, old Liz Williams had watched her husband, two sons and daughter die in succession. She was unable to light a fire, or bury the bodies, and fear of the dogs caused her stay in the house on her own for eleven days, living on berries and raw flour. Outside, the starving huskies, no longer being fed, tried repeatedly to gain entrance into the building. When rescued she was still sane and amazingly resilient.

At another small community, Dr Paddon found the only survivor was a seven-year-old girl, Martha Menzel. Like Liz Williams, she had survived on a diet of berries and raw flour, but unlike Liz was sharing the house with a pack of huskies. These dogs had no one to feed them but Martha had let them into the house as she had no fuel and needed to lie beside them and nestle against their bodies for warmth. Amazingly the dogs did not harm her, possibly because there was enough scavenging outside to keep them fed. She survived in this way for three weeks until friends came to investigate and rescue her. Despite her ordeal, Martha grew to womanhood and motherhood.[5]

The need to provide for these orphaned children was a task that Harry Paddon accepted. With his friend Henry Gordon, an Anglican priest, he established the Labrador Public Schools project. Harry financed the project with fundraising visits to New York, Boston, Ottawa and Montreal. He was not a natural speaker and did not like the task, but it was a necessary prelude to establishing the schools and dormitories they needed, and he went out and did the job. The first school was established at Cartwright with an English nurse-matron, English teachers and forty-four children in residence during the first school year.[6] The second school and residential dormitory took seven years to finance and build. It was located at North West River and seemed a happy place when Valerie and I settled there in September 1958. One recollection is of attending the barn dances that the children held in the residential block.

The Paddons

The service provided to the people of Labrador by Drs Harry and Tony Paddon was unique. With the assistance of Mina (Tony's mother) and a stream of volunteers from North America and the UK, they provided the medical service for the people of Labrador from 1912–78, working at times in the harshest of conditions and making long journeys to isolated communities, initially by dog team and boat, later by aeroplane. The father was the pioneer, but his son maintained and developed the practice as described by Cyril Goodyear in his report of life at Nain (entitled 'Unitas Fratrum') published on the internet in 2003. Having served in Europe during World War II, Goodyear returned to Canada and joined the Newfoundland Rangers. The duties of this force was similar to those of the Canadian Mounted Police, but because Labrador was not then part of Canada, but a region administered by the British Colonial Office, a clear distinction was maintained between the two police forces. Later they were amalgamated. Goodyear's first assignment was to Nain, a village on the north-east coast of Labrador. He says of that time:

> There were no roads anywhere in Labrador and few in Newfoundland. All travel was by ship, small boat, or dog team in winter. From the middle of October until the end of July the following year we never saw anyone from the outside world, except Dr Tony Paddon from the Grenfell Mission at North West River. He made one trip each winter by dog team. The only communication system we had, except for boat mail, was by Morse code equipment at the trading posts. Nain had only seven permanent families. The population of my district lived principally in the bays or fishing places, and visited Nain for trading and religious purposes. It was isolation that few can comprehend today. The Moravian missionaries – Bill Peacock,

his wife Doris and baby daughter – lived in the fenced missionary compound together with his predecessor the Reverend Paul and Mrs Hettasch. Their daughter Kate lived with them and ran the mission boarding school. Like her parents, Kate was educated in Germany and lived most of her life in north Labrador. All were fluent in the Eskimo language.

The Nain recorded by Cyril Goodyear has changed a great deal since those immediate post-war years. The nearby anorthrosite quarries have fuelled the economy and the village has grown from a small hamlet into a town of over 1,300 people. Of these, 340 are listed as school children in the 2003 census. The children can now choose to be taught in English or the Inuit language, the latter being an unlikely option when I was there in 1958. The town has its own TV channels, and radio broadcasts are made both in English and Inuktitut. These are developments that Dr Paddon would have encouraged and helped to secure, just as he helped to establish the first nursing station at Nain. When I visited the village it had only one nurse. Now the health centre has visiting dentists and doctors, at least five nurses, a laboratory technician, and various aides.

Conditions have changed in other ways: Dr Paddon first visited Nain by dog team and boat; I went by aeroplane, in a single-prop Beaver plane equipped with skis, floats and wheels so that it could land on ice, earth and water. I flew the 340 kilometres from North West River by a direct route, but Tony Paddon travelled more circuitously by dog team because he needed to visit other villages on his way to Nain. Due to the remoteness of the practice, we both had our moments of crisis. A radio call for help for an Inuit fisherman at Nain was a major problem for me, as he had gas gangrene of the leg which required amputation at St Anthony's Hospital in Newfoundland. This was difficult to arrange, as is described later in this chapter.

Tony Paddon had different situations to handle. When he arrived at Nain by boat, before aeroplanes became available, he was met by a distraught Bill Peacock. Bill's daughter was close to death with pneumonia but Tony saved her because he had salvaged some penicillin from a military plane that had crashed in one of the lakes and was able to treat the girl effectively. Antibiotics were so scarce in Labrador that they had to be conserved and used with great care. Tony made this clear soon after I arrived in North West River. He told me that 300,000 units of penicillin once a day was sufficient to treat an adult with lobar pneumonia. I had been taught to give a million units every six hours. I soon changed my practice.

Missionaries

Missionaries had an important role in caring for the Labradorean sick even in the 1950s. The IGA had a nursing station in two villages, at Nain and Happy Valley, but elsewhere missionaries acted as frontline medics, communicating with the hospital by radio-telephone. I did not go to church in Labrador but worked closely with the missionaries as well as the nurses at the IGA stations. There was a clear divide in the missionaries' responsibilities across the ethnic groups. The Inuit looked to the Moravians for pastoral care and help, the Innu to the Roman Catholic priests, and the settlers (known locally as liveyers) mostly to the United Church of Canada or the Pentecostal Church.

Moravians were the first Christian missionaries to visit Labrador. Their Church, an early form of Protestantism, was established by Jon Hus in the fourteenth century in Bohemia, which is now part of the Czech Republic. It is a small Church with about 850,000 members worldwide, but has been closely associated with the Inuit of Labrador for almost 300 years. Bill Peacock was the Superintendent of Moravian missions in Labrador when I was there. By then, he and his wife Doris had moved from the northern villages to Happy Valley in central Labrador where Doris was headmistress of a local school. They were a delightful couple, and in Hebron, anyone could walk into their house, day or night. Life in the valley was easier for them than in the north where conditions were more stringent. In those bleaker regions the missionary was expected to act as the local medical man. His duties included extracting painful teeth, and on one occasion Bill had to deal with a personal problem. He had the most awful toothache, and when he could no longer stand the pain, decided to extract the offending tooth. He managed to attach the dental forceps to the tooth but lacked the resolve the pull it out. Happily the dilemma resolved itself. When he loosened the forceps there was a slight release of pus and the pain eased.

Bill's predecessor, the Reverend Paul Hettasch, was a versatile man and a good surgeon. He had received some surgical training in Germany and was able to amputate digits, hands and arms whilst supervising inexperienced anaesthetists. He was known always as Dr Hettasch. On one occasion he removed a hand at wrist level with a Newfoundland Ranger giving the anaesthetic. The ranger involved, Cyril Goodyear, described him as a level-headed person who coped with emergencies in an unflappable way. I never met him but knew his children, Kate and Siegfried, who were the first children born of Moravian missionaries in Labrador that did not die in childhood. Siegfried and his family lived in a large prefabricated house, that had been built in Europe two hundred years earlier, transported to Labrador, then rebuilt in Hebron. He spoke fluent English, German and Inuktitut, and was possibly interned during the war. The stress of living in such an isolated place was apparent by the pressure on his speech on meeting someone from outside the area – he needed to talk incessantly. The living conditions of the Inuit at Hebron was unsanitary and dreadful. They lived in wooden huts with few facilities, in a sub-arctic climate. Siegfried took me to see a man with pneumonia, a young Eskimo who was sweating profusely and complaining of severe pain in the chest. He had pleurisy. The hut was warm but had little else to recommend it. Siegfried had given the man penicillin but had not thought of easing the pain. On my suggesting analgesics, he gave him some morphine. The patient's pain was so intense and conditions in the hut so bad that I thought of taking him back to North West River, but transferring him to the plane was too hazardous and it was safer to leave him where he was. I was relieved to learn later that he made a good recovery.

Like her brother Siegfried, Kate Hettasch was educated in Germany but spent most of her life in Labrador. She was a popular person in the region, an artistic spinster and a free spirit who seemed content with her dogs and her life with the Inuit. She lived in Makkovik and taught at the school when I knew her. It was a coastal village which was almost destroyed by fire a few years after I left Labrador. I did not see Kate again, but obtained news of her fifty years later when I was a voluntary guide at Coventry Cathedral. A Dutch visitor was looking for a collection box that the Moravian Church in Saxony had given to the cathedral when the building was consecrated in 1962. It was one of my favourite items in the cathedral, partly because of my association with the Moravians in Labrador and also because it was such a simple and appropriate gift. The box was made of wood, with a slot for donations and a wooden tripod for a base, somehow reminiscent of the widow's gift of her only mite. Sadly, I could not show my visitor the box because it had been vandalised and robbed for the few coins that it might have contained. A new box had been placed on the original site near the Chapel of Unity and I showed him this, but he was obviously disappointed by the vandalism. We talked about the work of the Moravian Church in Labrador and I mentioned Kate and Siegfried Hettasch. He knew Kate and reported that she was living in a home for retired missionaries in the Netherlands, but could give no information about Siegfried, perhaps because his circumstances were different as he had a wife and children.

I used to do clinics at the coastal villages. The missionaries would select the patients to be examined and I would see them in the missionary's house. Jeff, the pilot, would fly me into the village and tell me how long I could spend at the clinic, and then we would return to North West River with any patients that needed to be admitted to the hospital. Sometimes a light meal would be prepared, which the head of the house shared with me, but no other family member would be present. This reflected the poverty of Labrador's past when visitors would be given the best the family could afford but there would probably not be enough for everyone. I attended a clinic that was arranged by two Pentecostal missionaries and shared a meal with them afterwards. They were both young women, in their twenties or early thirties, and one looked the sickest person I had seen that day. She was obviously suffering from Grave's Disease, an overactive thyroid with swelling of the thyroid gland and exophthalmos, protrusion of the eyes. I suggested she sought medical advice in Newfoundland, but she was determined not to do so, preferring to put her trust in God's healing grace and in prayer to cure her. I did not see her again, so do not know if she eventually accepted the advice.

Two Catholic priests from Belgium resided in Labrador. They looked after and lived with the Innu (Montagnais-Indian) community. Fr Peterson was based at Davis Inlet, a miserable place which at that time had the highest suicide rate in the world. I went there only once and was not eager to repeat the visit. Harry Paddon described it "as the worst place, if there be a worst place, on the whole Labrador coast for winged pests in the summer season. You eat, drink, think, dream and talk mosquitoes and black flies... Davis Inlet is bad enough for me, and if there is a worse may I never go there."[7] The Innu lived in huts at Davis Inlet, but at North West River they lived in tepees, the traditional North American Indian tent. The tepees were heated with iron stoves and had the pleasant natural smell of wood from the forest. This Innu community was situated on the south bank of Lake Melville, almost directly opposite the hospital. They had their own church and school on the south bank, and were supervised by Fr Pirson, who had a reputation for strictness. Apart from physical differences, I observed two distinct differences between the Inuits and Innus. Whilst both had lost much of their cultural and spiritual heritage, the incidence of sexually transmitted disease was noticeably higher among the Inuit. On the other hand, the Innus always looked morose whilst the Inuit appeared cheerful.

Clinical Depression

No one in Labrador ever consulted me because they were depressed. This was not surprising as we had no effective treatment for depression, not even ECT. Talk therapy was a possibility, but in that case people would tend to consult their pastor or priest in preference to Dr Paddon or myself. Alternatively, they may have shared their inner problems with family or friends, or sought the help of a traditional healer – if so, I was not aware of it. In retrospect, I think it is possible that the Innu had an effective treatment for affective disorders at the time. Now that the use of sweat lodges by North American Indians is becoming more widely known, I was interested to read a report (internet – 4 August 2009) by Anna Davies (a medical student at the Memorial University, Newfoundland) of her experience in a sweat lodge at Goose Bay. She started with a short summary of her experiences in Labrador and of the social issues that she expected to encounter. Of the social issues she wrote: "Drug and alcohol abuse, suicide, unemployment, these rates are certainly higher on the coast than anywhere else I have ever lived." And of the sweat lodge, where initially she sat quietly for hours, she said: "In the sweat lodge, I heard myself sharing experiences... Everything I needed to get off my chest... came flooding out... When it was over a massive wave of relief and peace washed over me." I think it is likely that many depressed people would love to have such a sense of relief and peace engulfing them.

'Dancing in the Spirit' may be another way of managing depression in Newfoundland and Labrador. Its effectiveness as a therapy occurred to me on reading a report by R Ness, a sociologist, on the difference in emotional distress experienced by two communities living in the same Newfoundland village. Both groups belonged to a fundamentalist church. One was Pentecostal, the other was not. Ness found that emotional distress was less likely among members of the Pentecostal Church, and that the main difference between the churches was that the Pentecostal Church had regular healing services in which men 'Danced in the Spirit'. During the dances they gyrated frenetically around the church, before eventually rolling on the floor for several minutes and lying still. The other 'saints' then gathered around the individuals to hear the Spirit's message which they uttered, usually in tongues.[8]

North West River

Our base in Labrador was at North West River, a small community in central Labrador with about 500 people. Three ethnic groups lived there, the Innu, Inuit and settlers. The settlers were sometimes known as liveyers (pronounced "livers here"), a local name they used to distinguish themselves from more transitory residents, as they were a homogenous group whose European forebears had settled permanently in Labrador. The Innu lived on the south bank of Lake Melville whilst the Inuits and liveyers occupied the north side. They were separated by a fast-flowing neck of water which linked Lake Melville with the northern Grand Lake. The North West River community was quite isolated and could be reached from Newfoundland only by plane or boat.

The buildings on the north side of Lake Melville were built

mainly of timber. They included a church (United Reformed Church of Canada), a dormitory, a school, a Hudson Bay Company store and hospital. The hospital was a newly-constructed building with a well-equipped dental suite, but no dentist, and an equally well-equipped X-ray unit and pathology lab but no technicians to man them. Dr Paddon was in overall charge, but Jack Watts was the works manager and an English housekeeper did the catering. The nursing care was provided by two English nurses (Ellen and Sheila) assisted by young women from the local communities. Both nurses were trained midwives. Ellen also acted as anaesthetist when an operation required a general anaesthetic. The theatre had a modern anaesthetic machine which was never used. Instead, our patients were induced with vinesthene and kept unconscious with ether, with Ellen carefully dripping the anaesthetics on to a gauze mask that she held over the patient's face. Sheila was the theatre sister when we operated, and when Dr Paddon was away, my assistant surgeon was a young woman with no formal training. The nurses were very efficient. Both were hard-working and uncomplaining, and never seemed to have any time off. Nurses of similar dedication and calibre had always been employed by the IGA in its hospitals and nursing stations in Labrador, and many came from the UK.

The staff at North West River had much to teach me, starting with Tony Paddon who showed me how to extract teeth. This was a basic requirement in Labrador, as dentists, though highly prized, rarely visited the area and doctors were expected to have some dental skills. We did no conservation work, and someone was often waiting to have a tooth removed at the clinics we held in distant villages. Tony also taught me to remove a pterigium, perform a tonsillectomy and treat seal fingers, as will be discussed later. The nurses showed me around the laboratory and X-ray department. Taking X-rays, and undertaking blood and bacteriological tests were jobs they readily passed to me, for they already had enough to do in caring for the patients. The X-ray machine was up-to-date and versatile. It was designed for general practitioners in isolated practices, and its fixed settings enabled untrained medics to undertake a variety of X-rays and obtain good quality films. Most of our patients came from distant villages, and were brought in by air. Tuberculosis was such a major problem in the area that, when a new patient arrived, I would routinely take an X-ray of the chest downstairs before taking them to the wards upstairs. One patient who was in the hospital when I arrived was a boy recovering from diphtheria. He had a residual neuropathy and was the first case of diphtheria I had encountered since 1937, when I was admitted with diphtheria to an isolation hospital in Wales. In North West River, I soon learnt that Ellen and Sheila had already made sure that everyone in the locality was fully immunized as a result of this recent outbreak and I did not come across any other diphtheria cases whilst in Labrador.

Happy Valley

We arrived in Labrador just before the fall, when the autumn colours are most lovely. The winter snow was still to descend and weeks were to pass before the lakes froze hard enough for the snowmobiles, heavy as tanks, to take us across Lake Melville to Happy Valley, where the IGA had a nursing station with two beds. Happy Valley was the civilian town adjoining Goose Bay, an important USA Air Force (USAAF) base. The USAAF base had a well-equipped medical centre but was allowed to treat civilians, only if they worked on the base. All other civilians needing medical care were treated by the IGA. This was a puzzling arrangement, as we had few doctors and nurses, whilst Goose Bay had both the expertise and the facilities at hand, but it was not a decision we could influence. As mentioned, the International Grenfell Association was a medical charity established by Sir George Grenfell early in the twentieth century for the people of Labrador, and was funded by voluntary donations from Canada, the USA and the UK. By the 1950s the Newfoundland Government had become increasingly involved and paid for all the drugs needed to treat tuberculosis. It also provided a single-prop aeroplane for transporting patients, schoolchildren and staff across the territory. The government's involvement increased steadily until the late 1970s, when it agreed to pay for all the medical care in the region. Finally, in 1981, the IGA handed all its nursing stations, hospitals, equipment and land pertinent to the service over to the Newfoundland Government for the sum of $1. The charity maintains a commitment to the region by financing students from Labrador who wish to attend universities and other centres of higher education. In 2009, it awarded grants totalling $1,127,050.

In the winter months, I visited Happy Valley by aeroplane or snowmobile, but my first visit was in the fall. Then we used a less direct route. This involved crossing two stretches of water and travelling along a dirt track in two different vehicles. The first obstacle, the water flowing from Grand Lake to Lake Melville, was crossed in a dory, a flat-bottom rowing boat used by deep-sea fishermen off the coast of Newfoundland. At the other side, we transferred to a truck and drove through a pine forest to a river, which we also crossed in a dory. There, the IGA ambulance waited to take us to the nursing station at Happy Valley where Jo, the very efficient English nurse and midwife, ran the centre. Jo always had plenty of patients waiting to be seen at Happy Valley. If there were teeth to extract, we began with those, then I would fit any contraceptive diaphragms that were required. On my second visit, Jo produced a boy with acute mastoiditis, the first case I had seen, though I remembered various boys at school (all sons of doctors) who had mastoidectomy scars. The need to operate seemed compelling but I had never seen the operation done and knew I was not competent to attempt it. Dr Paddon was on holiday with his family in Bermuda and I was the only civilian doctor in Labrador. On discussing the situation with Jo, she very sensibly said, "leave him with me, I'll give him antibiotics and we will see how he does." By the following week she had cured him.

I did not like travelling in the snowmobile (it was too confined) but otherwise I liked going to Happy Valley partly for the food. Living close to an airbase, Jo could get items which were unobtainable elsewhere in Labrador, and sometimes she provided salad for lunch, which was a special treat. I think she preferred venison, which was readily available in Labrador, but deer meat was never a personal favourite of mine. Sometimes at North West River we were given fresh salmon, which Valerie used to fry and was absolutely delicious.

Settling In

One of Valerie's first tasks on our arrival in Labrador was to order the stores needed for the rest of the year. Much was obtainable from the Hudson Bay Store but perishable foods, like meat, had to be brought in by boat whilst the lakes were free of ice, and stored in the IGA's big freezer. She also had to meet her neighbours and settle into our new home. It was a newly-built house, but not quite complete when we arrived, so our first nights in Labrador were spent in the hospital's dental suite, which had its own bedroom and bathroom. Our neighbours lived close by as we shared the house with Jeff the pilot and his mechanic, Jerry. Jeff was born in Rhodesia and had flown fighter planes with the RAF in World War II. Here he flew a single-prop Beaver which Jerry, a local man, serviced and maintained. They had a good relationship and slept in the basement whilst we occupied the upper floor. They had their meals in the hospital whilst two female teachers shared an evening meal with us which Val cooked for them. I am not sure why this arrangement was made, as the teachers slept in another house. Val cooked on an Aga stove which would have been great if the correct fuel had been provided, but unfortunately, the coke was too large to keep it going overnight, and it had to be relit each morning. Despite these inconveniences, it was a contented household which Jimmy Toglavini, an Inuit boy, visited regularly for afternoon tea. He always came alone, and would stand outside the back porch, waiting quietly until he was invited in. On entering the house, he would take off his cap, sit down and join us at the table, saying nothing during the meal. Afterwards, with a brief thank you, Jimmy returned to the dormitory where he boarded during the school term, and we looked forward to his return the next day.

Of those who lived in the house, only Jeff required my medical help. His was a nocturnal emergency and we were all in bed when Jerry came to tell me that Jeff was in great pain. I went to find him sweating and in great discomfort. He had proctalgia fugax, a cramp-like pain in the rectum which, like any cramp, is self-limiting but very painful. I do not remember the treatment or advice given at the time but I did help a man with the same trouble much later in Warwickshire. He needed no treatment, his episode having occurred the previous night, but he came to consult me and I listened as he described the intense pain he had suffered that night. Not surprisingly he was very worried, but I was able to reassure him that the condition was harmless and no more sinister than a cramp in the leg. I told him also about Jeff having had a similar problem in Canada. Some thirty years later I was in a supermarket when this former patient came and spoke to me of the incident, and thanked me for the help I had given him so many years previously. I had done nothing; just listened and reassured him, and told him of Jeff's similar plight in Canada. Our meeting in the supermarket was only the second time we met, and I am often puzzled by the way people remember me over the years, but he was very grateful, and fortunately had no other bouts of proctalgia fugax.

Gas Gangrene

This is a tale of two men, a liveyer and an Inuit, but mainly of the Inuit. I do not know the latter's name but the liveyer was Jack Watts, a pivotal member of the IGA team in Labrador. Jack was born in Newfoundland in 1902 and joined the Canadian Marconi Company as a wireless operator in 1923. He was first posted to Makkovik, then to North West River and joined the IGA in 1928, remaining with the Grenfell Mission for the rest of his life. He was the Mission's general foreman and construction supervisor, which included supervising the building of the house and hospital in which I lived and worked in Labrador. Jack had various jobs before joining the Marconi Company, including as skipper of a fishing vessel and clerk in a store. He was a versatile man of great competence and inner strength. Fortunately he was in post when I arrived at North West River and helped to avoid a potential disaster which had its origin in Nain and was finally resolved in Newfoundland.

The crisis arose when Dr Paddon was on holiday. I had been in post for about four weeks when he left and was the only civilian doctor in Labrador. I learned of the crisis when I returned to the hospital from Happy Valley, and was told to contact the nurse at Nain immediately. We had good radio communications with the outlying stations so I was able to get in touch with her at once. She told me that an Inuit had shot himself in the leg while fishing, and was lying in her unit with a badly damaged limb. She had given him penicillin and tetanus antitoxin, but could not send him to hospital as the weather was bad and flying impossible. She wanted to know what else should she do? I advised her to give anti-gas gangrene toxin, but she had none, and to elevate the leg and ease the pain with analgesics, which she did. We agreed to speak in the morning and hoped that the weather would improve. That night, fearing that I might have to amputate the leg (an operation I had never seen performed), I studied *Bailey & Love's Short Practice of Surgery*, (my student's surgical textbook) for information on limb amputation, but the book gave no practical advice. The next morning we spoke again and I was told that the leg had become very swollen and discoloured. I needed to see the patient and Jeff agreed to fly me to Nain, but the weather turned nasty further north and he decided to fly back to North West River. So I went to the clinic at Happy Valley, probably by dory, truck and ambulance.

When I returned to the hospital, the weather at Nain had improved sufficiently for Jeff to fly north and return with the injured man. The airstrip at Nain was located outside the village, and the patient had been taken by sledge to the landing site before being placed inside the plane. At our next meeting, the nurse said she had slipped a small bottle of whisky into the man's pocket as an aid for the journey. She knew it was illegal to give alcohol to the Inuits, though under the circumstances, it was a kind and sensible thing to do. I saw him soon after he was admitted to hospital and his injury looked dreadful. The leg below the knee was swollen and black, it was obviously gangrenous, probably with gas gangrene. We gave him anti-gas gangrene vaccine and the need to amputate the leg was obvious, the only uncertainty being where and by whom it should be done. I contacted Dr Gordon Thomas, an experienced surgeon and head of the IGA at its base in St Anthony's Hospital, Newfoundland and we discussed the situation. I had already incised the tissues to relieve the tension in the leg, and this minor operation had produced the smell of mice, typical of gas gangrene. My only previous experience of this was at the Miners' Hospital, where a young married woman had died of gas gangrene following a miscarriage. Dr Thomas agreed that there was nothing more to be done at North West River that evening, and that the patient should be transferred to St Anthony's Hospital in the morning, if the weather was suitable for flying.

The next morning, the weather at North West River was turbulent, and there was no possibility of flying the patient to Newfoundland. I was thinking seriously of amputating the limb, though I doubted my ability to do so effectively, when Jack Watts walked into the theatre with two of his men. He said that the patient could be flown to St Anthony if taken to Goose Bay, where a twin-prop Otter aeroplane was based which could fly in conditions impossible for our single-prop Beaver. Jack made it clear that he intended to take the patient to Goose Bay. I watched as his men placed the man on a stretcher, carried him out of the hospital to the landing stage where the Beaver was floating on the water, and where Jack had prepared two dories, with the bow of one tied to the stern of the other. The patient, fully conscious and uncomplaining, was placed in the rear boat with Jack sitting in the stern to control and steer. His men seated themselves in the leading dory, and, at Jack's command, rowed both boats over the turbulent water. On reaching the far bank, the patient was transferred to a truck and driven through the forest to the river, which was also crossed by rowing boat. From there he was taken by ambulance to Goose Bay and placed in the two-prop plane. The flight to St Anthony's was uneventful and the leg was amputated by Dr Thomas. The man was provided with an artificial limb and six months later was fishing again off the coast at Nain.

The story did not end there. Twenty years later I received a copy of *The Deep Sea Fisherman*, the journal of the International Grenfell Association, and read of the next episode in the drama. The journal reported the case of an Inuit fisherman, who twenty years previously had suffered a gunshot wound in Nain, been admitted to the hospital at

North West River, and was transferred by Dr Paddon (an understandable error but it was Dr Rees) to St Anthony's Hospital where his leg was amputated. The report stated that the man had been re-admitted as an emergency to the hospital at North West River, this time with an acute abdomen. His condition was so poor that a surgical registrar was flown from St Anthony's to North West River to oversee his transfer to Newfoundland. This was accomplished and the man was admitted to St Anthony's Hospital and taken to theatre where a laparotomy was performed. The expected perforated appendix was not found. Instead the right psoas muscle was found to be gangrenous and was excised. It seems likely that the *Clostridia* bacteria had remained dormant in the leg for two decades, eventually tracking up into the psoas muscle before suddenly erupting. Again he made a full recovery and returned to Nain.

Sledge Dogs

The hospital porter at North West River was an elderly Inuit. He was a small man, probably not much more than five feet tall, and had lived most of his life above the tree line in the more barren parts of Labrador. He moved south when his wife became ill with cancer and was admitted to hospital, where she eventually died. He settled in North West River to be close to her, and soon became leader of the small Inuit community living there. In his youth he had been a renowned hunter and killed many seals and polar bears. It was said that if he encountered a polar bear, he preferred to kill the bear with an axe, and not with a gun. Asked why he preferred to get close to such dangerous creatures when he could kill them at a distance with the rifle, his reply was simple. He said, it is easy to kill a bear with an axe if the dogs are with you. They will trouble the bear so much that you can get close without it noticing and give it a lethal blow. Hunters need to conserve their bullets, because they are never sure when they may need them to kill seals or other creatures. I understand that the porter did not remain at North West River indefinitely but returned to his home further north. He would not have returned to an igloo; the Inuits I visited lived in wooden huts and I never saw an igloo in Labrador. Nor did I see anyone ski, except for a policeman visiting the northern villages. Skis were not used by Labradoreans in the 1950s, though snowshoes were sometimes used. I tried walking with snowshoes and found it very awkward, but they were useful in the forests where the snow was soft and deep.

A Canadian Mounted Police constable visited the villages routinely and shot any husky dogs that were not securely tethered. Some dogs were dangerous – for instance, the face of the 11-year-old son of the Moravian missionary based in Nain was badly scarred by a husky bite. The father, who was from England, had malignant hypertension and was forced to retire early from the mission field, though he was reluctant to go. On one occasion at Hebron, I decided to go for a walk across the ice, and on turning back found myself alone and close to a free-running pack of huskies. This was somewhat worrying but I managed to keep the dogs ahead of me and was mightily relieved to reach the village. Dog teams were still used at North West River when we were there, but I only once travelled on a dog sleigh. Soon after we arrived, I was told that a patient needed to be seen that night, and soon found myself sitting on a sledge with a large medicine chest, being rushed through the forest in the darkening light. The ride was swift, uncertain but quite exhilarating. I am not sure how I managed to stay on the sledge, but the excitement of the dogs as they raced amongst the trees remains a vivid memory. Of the patient I remember nothing, which I hope means that he or she was not seriously ill and made a speedy recovery.

Caesarean sections

We did two Caesarean sections at North West River. The first was by Dr Paddon with myself as his assistant; the second I undertook with a young Innu woman as my aide. Both were classical sections, with the front of the uterus being incised vertically through the thickest part of the uterine wall. This type of section is only performed by surgeons who lack the skill to undertake the less damaging lower segment sections. The first baby was delivered soon after I arrived at the hospital. The mother, an Innu, was brought by canoe from the settlement to the hospital at Lake Melville. She was in labour but walked all the way from the landing stage to the hospital, then up a flight of stairs to the maternity ward. Because she was in labour, and had had a previous classical Caesarean section, arrangements were made to operate immediately. This was necessary because a previous classical section increases the likelihood of the uterus rupturing, as happened to an emergency admission in the Miners' Hospital. The nurses soon had the theatre organised. Ellen gave the anaesthetic, Sheila acted as theatre sister, Dr Paddon was the surgeon and I was his assistant. The abdominal wall was stretched and thinned by the pregnancy, and once the abdomen was opened it was apparent that the uterus was beginning to rupture through the old Caesarean scar. Despite the urgency, there was no sense of crisis. The operation proceeded normally; the mother and baby did well and, after a short stay in the hospital, returned to the Innu settlement and to life in their tepee home. Innu and Inuit children were often brought to the hospital with respiratory infections and were always admitted; otherwise the mortality rate was high. Caring for the small children was quite a task for the nurses and their aides as the children's ward was always occupied.

I performed the second section when Dr Paddon was in Bermuda. This woman was not in labour on admission to hospital, but her pregnancy was well advanced and she was having episodes of painless vaginal bleeding, suggestive of a low lying placenta (praevia). This was a dangerous development and we needed to observe her carefully, so we kept her in bed but the bleeding continued and the presumptive diagnosis of placenta praevia became more certain. We could not assess the progress of the pregnancy, nor determine the position of the placenta by ultrasound as the technique was not available, so all decisions had to be based on my clinical judgement alone. Eventually I became sure that she had a low-lying placenta and that a Caesarean section was essential. When I informed the nurses, there was no dissent; they simply prepared the patient and the theatre for operation immediately.

Like Tony Paddon I could only attempt a classical section but this time there was no doctor to assist me; instead, an untrained Innu aide stood on the other side of the patient to help me. She was remarkably good and did all that was required of her. When the uterus was incised, there was much bleeding and we had to work fast, but the placenta was lying low in the pelvis and the decision to operate had been correct. The baby and placenta were delivered and handed to another aide. Ergometrine was injected into the uterine muscle to make it contract and reduce the bleeding, then the enormous gash in the wall of the uterus was closed with thick catgut sutures. That done, the rest of the operation could be completed more slowly. We were all delighted when it was over. We had a live baby and mother when there had been a possibility of one or both dying. In my working life, there have been few moments when I felt that a life was saved because I was there – that was one such occasion. It was of course a team effort, and I was largely dependent on Ellen, Sheila and the aides, but as I was the only surgically trained person present, it fell to me to undertake the operation. I wasn't a praying person then, but I did start the operation with a silent prayer for help. The operation was even recorded on videotape as Jeff had a video camera and asked permission to film the process. No one seemed bothered by Jeff being in the theatre, we got on with the operation and scarcely noticed him. The mother's consent was not sought. In fact, no consent forms for any operation at North West River were required or completed whilst I was there. We were too concerned with the situation being dealt with, and perhaps with the inadequacy of our skills.

Normal childbirth

Sometimes obstetrics is about uncertain pregnancies and difficult labours, but conception and birth are natural processes and most mothers manage with minimal help. Two births remind me of this truth and help to place this narrative within the context of the normality of life. The pregnancies recorded above were unusual but otherwise I never spent much time in the labour ward. In contrast, Ellen and Sheila were trained midwives who cared for the mothers in labour efficiently with little input from me. They did, however, ask for help on one occasion. A young woman who had been in labour for a long time was getting tired, and they decided that a forceps delivery was appropriate. They asked me to deliver the baby but, after seeing the mother, I said no because it did not seem imperative, and would be more appropriate to wait a little longer. It was the mother's first baby and the child arrived soon afterwards. I was pleased that we had been patient because it was Jack Watts' grandchild and I felt that he would prefer it to be a normal birth, though this did not influence the decision. Both mother and child did well.

The other child was born fifty years later in New Brunswick. I learnt of the birth by browsing on the web for data on the Paddon family and found that a daughter, named Sienna Rose Paddon, had been born in Monkton, New Brunswick to Tracy Lynn Spurrell and Michael Anthony C Paddon, on 12 February 2008. The birth was reported on a Newfoundland website which said that Rose was the granddaughter of Mrs Sheila (and the late Dr Tony) Paddon. Learning of Rose's birth made me feel closer to the Paddons because Sheila Paddon was pregnant when I was in North West River and I supervised her antenatal care. Sheila was a nurse and midwife, who had trained at the Prince of Wales Hospital in London during World War II, and was there during the London Blitz. Being able to relate in this distant way to the families of people I knew many years before helped to make general practice such a special vocation for me.

Hydatidiform Mole

I undertook the antenatal clinics at North West River. They were not big clinics, but I saw each mother at the appropriate stage of her pregnancy. One woman was particularly excited at being pregnant, it was her first baby and the father, an American airman, had asked her to marry him. So wedding bells were soon to ring. Ellen was with me when I first examined her, and I said to Ellen, "I think she may have a hydatidiform mole," almost forgetting the remark once it was made. Some weeks later, when I returned from a visit to Happy Valley, I found Ellen waiting to tell me that a pregnant woman had been admitted, adding "you were right about her". As it was obvious I did not realise what she was talking about, she said, "come up and see", and we went to the ward where the woman lay in bed. I saw nothing unusual at first, then Ellen drew back the sheets and all was apparent. The diagnosis of hydatidiform mole was correct. Blood-stained clusters of grapes seemed to be flowing from the vagina. The bleeding was not light and I was horrified. This was the first time I had encountered this condition and had been taught that the only treatment was a total hysterectomy, an operation I knew I could not even think of attempting.

Meanwhile, the patient was bleeding and losing blood. Something needed to be done urgently. We had no blood bank and if we needed to transfuse blood, we would have to find a donor and then cross match it. That was far beyond my competence. At least I could give her intravenous fluids. We had plasma in stock and I set up a plasma drip, one into each arm. At least fluid was flowing into the veins, hopefully as fast as it was running out of the uterus. This continued for a few hours until I could stand the tension no longer, then we gave her an injection of ergometrine, which acted like a charm. The vaginal flow was reduced to a trickle, and our fears that she might bleed to death slowly disappeared. By the next day, the blood loss was negligible but her haemoglobin level was low. We dealt with that by starting her on a course of oral iron but one other uncertainty remained. Was she going to develop a chorionepithelioma, a malignant growth that is sometimes a by-product of hydatidiform moles? Happily, the likelihood of it developing could be readily assessed even in distant Labrador. Blood was sent for testing to the specialist laboratories and the reports came back negative. She was not going to develop that particular cancer. So the outcome was partly happy but not entirely. The marriage ceremony was put on hold and later cancelled, so she lost a prospective husband as well as her child.

Acute surgery

My surgical skills were very limited. After I qualified, I did no surgical internship and never assisted at an operation to remove an acutely inflamed appendix, but I was confident in my ability to diagnose those emergencies accurately. The test came when Dr Paddon was away. I saw two patients with acute appendicitis, a teenage boy and a married woman. Both were seen at the Happy Valley clinic, and Jeff brought them to the hospital in his Beaver. The boy's operation was straightforward though I did not perform the operation in the standard way, through McBurney's Point, but by a right paramedian incision which gives better access to the

Me as captain of the rugby team at Llandovery College, 1947

North West River, Labrador, Canada in the 1950s. Photograph shows the hospital and school and mission buildings

North West River Hospital in the mid 1950s. The landing stage is in the foreground

Doctor with pilot and white medical box at Rigolet Wharf in 1961

Nain harbour in 1961

Nain at dusk

Beaver plane and pilot docking to pick up passengers in 1962 at North West River

Coastal boat, the *Hopedale*, in Makkovik harbour in 1962

An Inuit community in Makkovik in 1961

Innu (Indian) children in Happy Valley by the Churchill River in 1961

Jack Watts' house in the 1950s

Log house in North West River in the 1950s, probably built by Dr Tony Paddon and his brother Harry

Valerie and I at Butlins Camp, Pwllheli for a Bangor Diocesan Conference in 1964

Abernant, Llandiloes. The surgery suite was to the right of the house

The David Davies Hunt
meeting outside Abernant
c.1964

Llanidloes Cottage Hospital

Valerie as deputy mayor of
Llanidloes with Eric Jervis
(mayor) and Gareth Morgan
(councillor) c.1972

Broneiron, the war time home of Gordonstoun School in the 1940s. Now a centre for Girlguiding Cymru (2011)

Clywedog Dam with disused tin mines in the foreground (2011)

Llyn Clywedog (2011)

Archimandrite Barnabus (third priest from the left) with other priests outside his house in New Mills, Powys on St Elias day in 1986

A cartoonist's impression of the waiting room in Stretton in 1980. A gift from the artist when I was moving to the hospice in Birmingham

abdominal contents. His recovery was uneventful and he returned home fit and minus his appendix.

I was sure that the woman also had an acutely inflamed appendix, the findings were typical. She had right lower abdominal pain and was tender in the right lower abdominal quadrant. Ellen and Sheila prepared the theatre and the patient was anaesthetised, then I picked up the scalpel for the first incision. Again I did not attempt the standard approach, through McBurney's Point, but entered the abdomen by a right paramedian incision which is commonly used in gynaecological surgery. It was fortunate that I did so. When I exposed the appendix, it appeared normal and not inflamed. The patient did not have an acute appendicitis. So I looked deeper into the pelvis and found the right fallopian tube. It was like a black sausage, black, swollen and looking very nasty. The patient had acute salpingitis, an infection of the fallopian tube. I had never seen anything like it, nor had I seen a patient with acute salpingitis before. I might have been tempted to excise the tube, but remembered the advice given by a surgical registrar when I was a medical student at St Thomas's. He said, "If you go into the abdomen to investigate a case of acute appendicitis, and a black sausage comes out of the pelvis, do not be tempted to cut it off. Leave it alone, otherwise she will die." I left it alone, replaced the fallopian tube in the pelvis, and closed the abdomen. When the woman was back in the ward, I started her on Chloramphenicol, a most effective broad spectrum antibiotic but one banned now because of its toxic effect on the bone marrow. My patient had a stormy convalescence, made worse by a right pleurisy, but she made a full recovery and returned home in good health. Before she left, I had one duty to discharge. It was important that she and her husband knew that the appendix had not been removed. They were disappointed and surprised when informed, but there was no recrimination and for that I am grateful.

Cold surgery

Very occasionally I was expected to treat a person with a pterygium, a condition I had not seen in the UK. A pterygium is a triangular growth of the conjunctiva that spreads from the inner side of the eye towards the pupil. It is benign and rarely interferes with vision, but it can do so, and Tony Paddon showed me how to remove it. The method is simple. Local anaesthetic is applied to the eye, then the pterygium excised and its severed edges sutured together with fine thread. My patients were always men, probably because their eyes were exposed more often that women's to the harsh weather conditions that cause the problem in Labrador.

Tony also taught me to perform a tonsillectomy, an operation I had no desire to do under any circumstance. It is an operation that I consider unnecessary, and dangerous if a trained anaesthetist is not present. I had no choice, it was a case of seeing one tonsillectomy done by Tony and doing the next myself. Fortunately, Sheila and Ellen were with me, and they were more experienced than I. Ellen anaesthetised the child with ether, and I dissected the tonsils from their bed and removed them with a guillotine. I was glad when the procedure was completed and the patient had survived, but sorry for the lad afterwards as he had such a sore throat.

Seal fingers were not a problem requiring surgery when I was in Labrador, but it was not always so. In Dr Harry Paddon's time, seal fingers were sometimes amputated, though rarely by him. The exact cause of seal fingers is not known but it is probably bacterial in origin. The trouble usually starts with a cut or abrasion on the hands of people who have contact with seals or their pelts. The affected fingers become swollen, painful and chronically inflamed. There is no pus to drain, but the joints may stiffen. Rest, hot fomentations, elevation of the arm and removal of the finger were used to treat the problem before antibiotics became available. Now the infection responds rapidly to antibiotics, tetracycline being the drug of choice in my time.

A Domestic Crisis

Not all the demands on my time were strictly medical. Tony Paddon and his father were both magistrates and represented the law in a region where the police force was largely invisible. The respect given by Labradoreans to their doctors was amazingly high (though in the case of the Paddons well deserved) and I was not greatly surprised when I was asked to intervene in a family dispute. The request to visit began with a knock on the door, and my presence was required because a young man was threatening to shoot another member of the family. I was not keen to go out into the night, but I collected my medical bag and accompanied the messenger to the water's edge where a canoe waited to take us to the other side. On the other side of the lake it seemed a long walk to the house, but before we arrived a messenger came and told us that the crisis had been resolved. So we retraced our steps and I returned home wondering how I would have coped if the situation had escalated. I had a chance to find out some years later in mid Wales, where I was asked to deal with a similar situation at the request of the local police sergeant.

A Cold Autopsy

I did not expect to do a post-mortem at North West River but I was given little choice. A man had died in the wilderness and his frozen corpse had been brought to the hospital and placed in a workshop. Dr Paddon was away and I was told that the police wanted an autopsy and that I was expected to do it. We had no post-mortem room, nor the instruments needed for making an autopsy, and I should have refused to be involved but that possibility did not occur to me. The body lay on a workman's bench and I went into the room alone to attempt the impossible. The body was frozen hard and I was provided with just a few surgical instruments and a workman's saw. I knew nothing about the man though guessed he was about 30 or 40 years old. There were no suspicious marks on the skin, so I opened the chest and abdomen and looked inside. I found nothing unusual because I did not know what to look for. Finally, I sutured the wounds and declared that he had died from natural causes, which seemed to satisfy everyone.

Like all medical students of my era, I had to dissect a human corpse and satisfy my examiners that I had a thorough knowledge of its anatomical structure. I spent two years studying anatomy in that way. My professor was a Welshman, Professor Davies, who I was to meet twenty years later in Llanidloes where his father was a patient of the practice. The professor was a slightly intimidating man, which was most noticeable at the end of our first term when we were examined on our term's work. Our subject was the upper limb. One corpse had been allotted to each table of six students and we worked as two teams, three friends working on the right arm and the others on the left. At the viva we were assessed as a table of six, each student being questioned separately.

Professor Davies examined my table and I was the last person to be questioned. He asked me to describe the pulp of the finger but my knowledge was so limited (in fact I knew nothing about the pulp of the finger) that the professor wanted an explanation for my ignorance. There was a perceptual tension around the table but I had my answer ready. I said that I had looked carefully in our dissecting manual – a book by Cunningham – for the information he wanted but there was nothing in it; then I had looked carefully in *Gray's Anatomy*, the standard text book of anatomy, which also said nothing about the pulp of the finger. Professor Davies didn't say a word, he got up and walked out of the room, and came back with a copy of *Gray's Anatomy* in his hand. Then, without saying anything, he gave us our marks. We all received the highest grade awardable, the only table to do so. At the time, Professor Davies was the editor of *Gray's Anatomy* so I was quite pleased to surprise him at the viva. I have not seen the later editions of *Gray's Anatomy* but I think it probable that they do say something about the pulp of the finger.

Farewell to Labrador

Our year in Labrador was a seminal experience for Valerie, Eileen and myself. I had wanted to work as a general practitioner in testing conditions and certainly achieved it. My experience of medical practice was enhanced and ability to cope with unexpected crises tested. As a family, we lived closely with people whose backgrounds differed greatly from our own, and our year in the sub-arctic may have inspired Eileen, many years later, to work in the conservation of water birds which breed in arctic and sub-arctic regions. Among my happiest memories is Eileen's first glimpse of a Christmas tree. It was a tree brought into our house by two young men on Christmas Eve, and she first saw it on entering the sitting room on Christmas Day. Delight illuminated her face, and she still remembers the experience. Valerie seemed very much at home in Labrador. The simple lifestyle suited her, she was at ease with the staff and children in the nearby dormitory, and was soon asked to help older children with their mathematics, which she did gladly. Val seemed quite content with North West River; only one thing began to worry her. She wished to extend our family and it was not until we returned to the UK that Anna was born.

The nights were not busy but I knew I could be called

out at any time, day or night. When visiting distant villages, I would spend the occasional night there, but we had only one night away from North West River as a family. It was a delightful surprise when Jeff told us one morning that we were to be flown to a log cabin in the wilderness that day. We were given no time to prepare and soon found ourselves in the Beaver, skimming over the trees until Jeff landed the plane on a lake close to the cabin. We clambered out of the plane and Jeff left, saying he would be back in a few days. But it was not to be so, he returned the next day saying I was needed at the hospital. Perhaps it was just as well because we had a sleepless night, the cabin had no mosquito nets and the insects were busy. Despite the mosquitoes, we would have liked out brief holiday to be longer. I have no idea what we ate, but we had food with us and Valerie probably built a fire and cooked on the beach by the lake. The sense of aloneness was great and the possibility that a bear might emerge from the landscape passed through my mind, but we saw no living creature except a few birds flying overhead. Val wanted to go skinny dipping. I wasn't keen because the water was cold and I am a poor swimmer but in we went and I am glad that we did. The next morning, we flew back to North West River where Tony Paddon was waiting to operate on a man with a peritonitis and needed my help. Unfortunately, he died on the table; we were all upset but nothing was said, as tended to be the custom in those days.

A few weeks later I called at the Paddons' house, as I needed to tell Tony that I had admitted a child with acute appendicitis. I can remember saying to him, "I've just seen Harry Ben and brought him in to the hospital with acute appendicitis." Tony thought that I was referring to an Inuit lad called Harri Ben and I had to correct him. "No," I said, "I mean Harry Ben Paddon, your brother's son." I've always admired his response. He accepted unflinchingly the responsibility of operating on his own nephew that night. I assisted him, whilst Ellen and Sheila carried out their usual tasks in the operating theatre, and all went well. Some years later, when we were resettled in the UK, young Harry Ben and his mother stayed with us in our home in mid Wales, as did Bill Peacock and his wife Doris.

4

Psychiatry in Wales
1959–60

Whitchurch Hospital

ON OUR RETURN to the UK we stayed, as usual, with Valerie's parents in Whitchurch, Cardiff. My own parents would have loved us to be with them, but Val was close to her mother, and gran's house had a large garden where a child could play. So as my parental home in Barry had no garden, on balance it was better that we stayed at Whitchurch. Moreover, there were other children in the house for Eileen to play with – her cousins Richard and Hilary, and Peter, the maid's son – whilst Eileen and Mike Roberts also lived in the house. Eileen was Val's widowed sister-in-law, and Mike was her second husband. He was a popular man who became head of the Bishop of Llandaff School in Cardiff, moved into politics and, having spent a few years as Assistant Whip whilst in opposition, became a Minister of State for Wales in the Thatcher government. Sadly, he died very suddenly whilst speaking at the dispatch box in the House of Commons. The two other Cardiff MPs, Jim Callaghan and George Thomas, were very supportive; the three men had been good friends even though their political views differed. 'FJ', as Val's father Fred was called, was also a well-known teacher in Cardiff, being president of the National Union of Teachers in 1954.

We had saved some money in Labrador and I needed a holiday and wanted to go to Paris with Val for a few days. But, she was not keen to go, saying that gran thought I should find another job, which I was quite happy to do. In those days, there was almost no specific training for general practice, but I knew work as a GP would be enhanced by experience in psychiatry, and a leading psychiatric hospital was just ten minutes' walk from the house. So I contacted Dr Hennelly, the medical director of Whitchurch Hospital, to ask if I could attend to learn some psychiatry. He arranged for us to meet, we had a brief chat and he asked Dr Spillane, a consultant psychiatrist, to show me around the hospital. I must have seemed acceptable for, a few days later, Dr Hennelly told me he had an SHO post available and suggested that "I go on to the books". This suited me, so I was given a white coat and started my career as a junior psychiatrist.

Whitchurch Hospital was originally named the Cardiff City Asylum. It opened in 1908 on a site that was sufficiently large for trustees to advertise for a farm foreman (working farm bailiff) to manage the grazing farm. His wages were £2 per week, with an unfurnished house and free water rates and taxes. This was considerably more than the wages paid to the south Wales miners which, at the time, was regarded as a well-paid workforce. In 1959, the hospital was a particularly good place to train in psychiatry. The Ministry of Health had described it as one of the three leading psychiatric hospitals in the country, and it was certainly an innovative centre. Unlike most psychiatric units in the 1950s, the wards were not locked but open; group therapy had been introduced and the use of halfway houses was being discussed. A Medical Research Council unit was located in the hospital, which probably enhanced the hospital's status. There was a good mood in the doctors' mess and registrars had a high expectation of reaching consultant status. One junior colleague became a professor at Cambridge University. Although my status was low and there was no specific training provided, I was made to feel a capable member of the staff and was put in charge of the men's medical ward in this large psychiatric hospital.

Sensory Deprivation

An elderly man, who was admitted fighting mad, is one of the patients I remember best. He was powerfully built and difficult to control, so we had to sedate him with the strongest drugs available, probably chlorpromazine or promazine. Eventually, he quietened down but remained unpredictable, which his family said was unusual as he was normally an even-tempered person. Such a change in personality suggested the presence of a brain tumour but he had no organic lesion, though he was very deaf. This was particularly interesting as a paper had just been published by researchers at McGill University reporting one of the earliest studies of sensory deprivation. At McGill University, volunteers had entered a tub of water, which was kept at body temperature to reduce sensory input through the skin. Their eyes were covered and white music played through earphones to reduce visual and auditory sensations. Within a few hours the subjects reported a loss in their sense of reality, they had hallucinations, bizarre thought patterns, and distortions in time and imagined space. I wondered if this might be a factor in my patient's strange behaviour, so I examined his ears and found them full of wax. It took a day or so to wash them out but eventually the ears were clean and he regained his normal hearing. He also regained his previous pleasant personality, and it was a joy to send him home, fully recovered and without medication. After that experience I never hesitated to examine a patient's ears and, if wax was present, always washed them out myself. It is a job I never delegated to anyone else.

Acute Anxiety

Another memorable patient was admitted in an acute anxious state. He was a well-dressed man, aged about thirty, who had been seen at home by a consultant and advised to come into hospital. His problems began after he had consulted his general practitioner with a skin rash, and was referred to a dermatologist for advice. Somehow he had managed to read the specialist's letter to the GP and found that the dermatologist had suggested that he might be schizophrenic. This possibility frightened him so much that the GP asked a psychiatrist to see him at home and the man was admitted to our unit as a voluntary patient. He was very anxious when I saw him, believing that he might be psychotic and dreading a night on the ward. Luckily, I had enough self-confidence to assure him that he was not schizophrenic and need not stay in the hospital unless he chose to do so. He left immediately. I heard no more of him until a few months later, when I was walking along St Mary's Street in Cardiff, a passing stranger stopped and thanked me for what I had done for him at Whitchurch Hospital. It was this former patient who had recognised me even though our previous meeting had been brief. He said that everything had gone well for him since leaving the hospital, he had regained his confidence and life was good again. I was pleased for him and noted, without comment, that he looked smarter and more self-confident than I did at the time.

Death in the Theatre

One patient I remember with sadness. He had been in the hospital for some years with chronic schizophrenia and I was asked to see him because he was complaining of recent abdominal pain. When I examined him it was obvious that he had peritonitis, probably from a perforated peptic ulcer. We informed the hospital's visiting consultant surgeon and he sent a senior registrar to confirm the diagnosis and, if necessary, to arrange for the man to be treated surgically. This the registrar did. In many psychiatric units he would have been transferred to a district hospital, but Whitchurch Hospital had its own operating theatre and the registrar arranged for the operation to be done at Whitchurch by the consultant surgeon with a consultant anaesthetist in attendance. First, the patient had to be informed and his permission given. It was my job to tell him that an operation was absolutely necessary, as initially he refused to go under the knife, but I persuaded him and he changed his mind. Later that day I accompanied him into the operating theatre, where I scrubbed up to help the surgeon with the operation. The man was anaesthetised and the surgeon made his initial incision, but the anaesthetist said, "His heart has stopped". There was no panic, everyone remained calm, the surgeon opened the thorax and massaged the heart until it began to contract again. Then he closed the incisions in the chest and abdominal wall, and the patient was returned to the ward. The peritonitis had not been treated and we all knew the man would die. I was with him when he recovered consciousness and he said to me: "I will be alright now won't I doctor, I did what you said." I can't remember my reply, but he died within two days. I did not tell anyone about it for many years. You don't take home incidents like this and share them with your wife and family. Maybe it would be better if one did.

Dark Night of the Soul

My first few weeks at Whitchurch Hospital were great. I got on well with my colleagues and had no difficulty in adapting to my life in psychiatry. In fact I seemed a natural for the job as I was a good listener and empathised easily with most patients. Then suddenly things went wrong, not in my work but within myself. I became extremely depressed and anxious. At night, alone in bed, I would just shake and tremble. Valerie was brilliant. Although I had always insisted on separate beds she would lie alongside me and hold me tight as I trembled uncontrollably. In the morning I would go to work and deal with the problems of the anxious, depressed and psychotic as usual. I decided I was suffering from an agitated depression, though post-traumatic stress disorder would be a possible diagnosis now, particularly as my spell in Labrador had been very stressful and had included the death from peritonitis of a man on the operating table. I knew that I could not handle the situation alone, so I telephoned Dr Spillane and arranged to meet him. He was very kind and sympathetic, and said that I was suffering from an anxiety state and that it augured well for my future in psychiatry. I was glad that I spoke to him but knew I was not cured. My inner state remained desperate but no treatment was offered or desired. I knew that I could see Dr Spillane whenever I wished but we never discussed the problem again.

In my studies I was not attracted to the teachings of Sigmund Freud, but the ideas of Carl Jung appealed to me as being more realistic and interesting. In particular, I was struck by the advice he gave to many of his patients. He told them that "the only cure for an affective disorder is a conversion to a religion of light", and advised them to resume the religious practices they had abandoned. Like most of my contemporaries, I no longer went to church and had become an agnostic. The Christian creeds which I had recited in my youth were no longer an acceptable statement of faith for me, but in my desperation I started going to church again on Sunday evenings, and found some comfort in doing so. Valerie and my parents-in-law were surprised but said nothing, and I continued to go to church each Sunday, being careful not to recite the creed with the rest of the congregation. Then slowly I found that I could say bits at the end and eventually, over a longish period of time it all made sense, and the recitation of the creed became an important part of my spiritual life.

Other factors helped my recovery. Valerie of course. Playing tennis also helped as the physical exertion enabled me to release repressed thoughts and feelings. With hindsight, I think that the rapid eye movements associated with tennis may have been useful as it mimicked to some extent the EDMR (eye movement desensitisation and reprocessing) used to treat people with post-traumatic stress disorders. If that assessment is correct, table tennis may have been even more helpful than tennis, as the flight of the ball changes more frequently and swiftly than in tennis.

The passage from the dark days of autumn to the lighter days of spring were also beneficial. So a year passed, I was much better and had to make a choice; did I want to stay in psychiatry or return to general practice? By this time I was confident that I would become a consultant psychiatrist if I wished, but I also knew my real intention was to return to general practice. One deciding reason was the increased possibility of treating the anxious and depressed at home. New psychotropic drugs had become available, most significantly phenelzine and imipramine that could be prescribed by the general practitioner. Also, Valerie had given birth to Anna, our second child, in gran's house. I was the duty doctor the night she was born, and when I was notified of Anna's birth I walked through the empty streets of Whitchurch in the early morning to see my new daughter and radiant wife. The likelihood of returning to general practice had become increasingly certain.

Jews and Gentiles

Despite my 'dark night of the soul', as one colleague described it, the work given to me was increased, not diminished. I was given a regular outpatient clinic at the City General Hospital, and a weekly session in child psychiatry, also at the same hospital. But most of my work was done at Whitchurch Hospital where some patients remain in my memory despite the passing years. One was a Jewish cabinet maker who enjoyed life in the hospital so much more than in the community that we used to protect him from being discharged home. He was a skilled craftsman and a good organiser and was always willing to help other men in the craft shop. One day he told me that he had a piece of oak that would make an excellent coffee table, and that he would like to make one for me. There would be no charge except to cover the cost of the wood. I said "yes, great, thank you". Fifty years later I still have the table, and though much battered, it remains in constant use.

Some patients in the hospital were people I had met in my normal social life, though I did not recognise them at the time. One was married to a distant member of my wife's family and we would pass each other in the hospital's corridor without exchanging a word. There was no clinical involvement between us and, at our subsequent social meetings, we never spoke of that transitory phase in our lives. Another patient was suffering from intense anxiety. This followed his engagement to the daughter of a Pentecostal minister who I had known in my teens. Whenever she visited him she was beautifully dressed and looked ravishing. I could understand him being attracted to her but he was not a religious man and did not want to marry the girl, but did not know how to escape the commitment he had made. Another patient was a Jew whose young wife asked to see me. She was a gentile and in a moment of altercation he had attempted to spank her, but she was a spirited woman and would have none of it. He became depressed, but his main problem was that he had married outside the faith, against the wishes of the family, and they had declared him dead. They were Orthodox Jews and had conducted the Jewish mourning rite of Shiva in his absence, so it was not surprising that he was unhappy and upset. But he was an able and determined man who would probably cope well eventually. Only once did I suggest to a patient that he might consider resuming the religious practices he had discarded. He was a student from the Middle East, attending Cardiff University, and had been brought up in the Catholic faith. He rejected my suggestion quite forcibly. I never made that suggestion again and have no interest in converting other people to my own beliefs.

Hidden Fury

Some patients were remarkably taciturn. I remember a consultation I had with an intelligent man suffering from schizophrenia. The session seemed to go well but after we left the consulting room and went our separate ways, I felt as if a dagger had been plunged suddenly into my back. It was such a powerful sensation that it caused me to turn around, only to see the man glaring at me malevolently. Nothing was said, we looked at each other, then continued in our different directions. We never met again. Another man was a refugee from Yugoslavia. He had settled in the UK after World War II and worked for many years in a Welsh coalmine. He was depressed and withdrawn and I never learnt what really troubled him. He had minor difficulties with the English language but his problems probably stemmed from the war, in which he had fought with the Royal Yugoslavian Army, initially against the Germans and later against the communists led by Marshall Tito. During this civil war the antagonism existing between the two opposing Yugoslavian forces was vicious and intense. The communists were victorious and my patient may have been lucky to escape to the West alive. I suspect that the horrors which he experienced and perhaps committed during the war continued to haunt him for the rest of his life but remained bottled up within him. Later, in Birmingham, I had the same impression when I was asked to see a terminally-ill man from the Baltic states who had fought with the German army, possibly with the notorious SS divisions, and then escaped to the West and settled in the United Kingdom. He was also withdrawn, taciturn and unwilling to talk about the past. Again I suspected that the horrors of the war and perhaps of what he had done could not easily be eradicated from his memory, nor openly expressed. This might have been the best coping mechanism for him, because a study of holocaust survivors has shown that the people who adapt to their new life best are often those who speak least of their past life.[9]

Abuse and Depression

I worked almost exclusively with male patients at Whitchurch Hospital. My involvement with female patients was restricted to the occasions when I was the resident physician at night and weekends, and I remember only two women patients clearly. Both were admitted as emergencies and I saw them because the hospital required each new admission to be examined by a doctor. One was a middle-aged woman who was a Quaker, a member of the Society of Friends, as was her husband. I did not expect to find anything unusual, and was surprised to see that she had extensive bruising on her buttocks. It was obvious that she had been severely beaten. When questioned she said that she had fallen downstairs, a common response from women with bruising on the face or exposed limbs. It was not my responsibility to determine the truth that night; that was the concern of the doctor who would see her in the morning. However, she remains in my mind as the first woman that I saw as a patient who was a victim of domestic violence.

The other woman was depressed and suicidal. She was determined to kill herself and had swallowed five-hundred aspirin tablets before being brought to Whitchurch Hospital. Ours was not the best place to bring her, as we were not geared to deal with medical problems or life-threatening emergencies, and in Cardiff such cases were taken usually to a general hospital. More bewildering, the lady lived in Bridgend and the ambulance had bypassed two hospitals to bring her to Whitchurch. But once she was admitted it was my job to make sure she survived, and she was in a bad state physically and emotionally when she arrived. I set up drips in both arms and washed out her stomach. There was mess everywhere but she did not die. My consultant had been warned and came to see what was happening. He seemed satisfied with his assessment and left me to continue the rescue work I had begun. The lady survived the night and in the morning became the responsibility of another doctor. I learnt that she swore she would try to kill herself again; I never knew the final outcome.

One other incident remains in my mind. One weekend, when I was the duty doctor, a sister on the women's wing came to me because she had a problem with one of her patients. She took me to the ward to see the woman who was cowering in a corner of a padded room. Sister told me that she had asked the doctor responsible to prescribe a tranquilliser but he/she had not done so. Later the woman had attacked her and, in defending herself, she had given the patient a 'good hiding' and placed her in a single room. She wanted me to prescribe a sufficient sedative to keep the woman quiet. I did so without comment. The sister was a slender woman, she was obviously upset and had dealt with a difficult problem alone as best as she could.

All this happened fifty years ago. Now Whitchurch Hospital is scheduled to be closed and its in-patient psychiatric service is to be transferred to Llandough Hospital, which I remember being built in the 1930s. No doubt the NHS will make a great deal of money when it sells the site, and efforts will be made to integrate the patients into the community, but I wonder if this was always the best policy for patients in the past? It may have been the right outcome for many people but I am not sure that it has been an overall success. At Whitchurch, most patients were admitted on a voluntary basis, and only a few had no legal right to leave. The general standard of care was high and chronically mentally/emotionally disabled people were not often found on the streets in parlous conditions as many do now. As beds were closed in the former psychiatric hospitals, many patients who were discharged moved onto the streets and into prisons. The UK now has the largest prison population in Europe and its inmates include a high proportion of drug addicts and the mentally ill. Prison seems an even less appropriate place for such people than the old mental hospitals. One last thought. When I retired I became a counsellor at a Young Offenders Institute and found that a surprisingly high proportion of these young people had suffered severe bereavements early in life. I learned, from my discussions with them, that they had been given little or no help in those early days when they needed it before drifting almost automatically into crime. Adequate bereavement support for these youngsters must be a better option than not dealing with the problem, and there needs to be a real sense of urgency in providing such support.

5

General Practice
in Rural Wales 1960–74

MY YEAR IN psychiatry had taught me a great deal about myself, and about the many inner problems with which people have to contend, but as parents our immediate focus was on re-establishing a separate home for ourselves and the children, which meant my returning to general practice. Two jobs caught my eye in the advert pages of the *British Medical Journal.* Both offered an assistantship with a view to partnership in well-established practices, and an unfurnished house/bungalow with the job. I applied for both posts. One was in Stamford in Lincolnshire, the other in Llanidloes, Montgomeryshire. The Stamford practice contacted me first, and invited me and Valerie for interview. The meeting went well and their bungalow seemed very desirable. If they had offered me the job then I would have accepted it, but the interviewers could not make a final decision as their senior partner was on holiday and his agreement was needed. Instead, I went to Llanidloes, which probably suited us much better. We met the partners, Tom Brittain and Graham Davies in Abernant, Graham's house, and they invited me to join them as an assistant. We agreed that I was to receive a fixed salary for 12 months, then a quarter of the practice income for five years and a full share subsequently. I also agreed to buy Abernant when Graham and his wife were ready to vacate it. In the meantime, I was to have the free occupancy of Dyfnant, a detached house overlooking the Clywedog valley in the heart of Wales. The location of the house and practice was idyllic. We were very contented there.

My Future Partners

Tom Brittain was the younger of the two partners but still a lot older than me. He began life as a junior civil servant, then studied medicine at Liverpool University and was drafted into the army during World War II. He was a competent anaesthetist, who had landed in Normandy soon after D-Day, advancing across northern Europe with the British Army as a captain in the Royal Army Medical Corps. After the war he married a Welsh nurse, Eirlys, and joined Graham at Llanidloes, living in Castle House where he had his own surgery and dispensary. They had three sons. The eldest became a GP, the second son a solicitor, and the youngest a headmaster. Tom was a quiet, pleasant man. He was a craftsman and an excellent woodworker. His main interest, apart from his family and work, was the Rotary Club which he helped to establish in Llanidloes and was its first chairman. Although the town had a very active branch of the British Legion, he never joined it, nor for that matter did Graham or myself, though we were all ex-servicemen. Graham Davies was in his early sixties when I joined the practice. He was more extrovert than Tom and had attended the same school as myself, Llandovery College in Carmarthenshire. He liked my having worked in Labrador with the Grenfell Association as its founder, Sir Wilfred Grenfell, was one of his early heroes. As a schoolboy he wanted to join the Royal Flying Corps during World War I, but the casualty rate was so high that his mother made him promise not to do so. Instead, he went to London aged seventeen and joined the London Scottish Regiment serving on the Western Front as a machine gunner. In 1917 he was posted to the newly formed tank regiment and sent back to England to be trained and commissioned as a tank commander. That posting may have saved his life as many young men were killed in the last fierce battles of the war. In 1919 he contracted the Spanish Flu, survived and went to Guy's Hospital to study medicine.

The following information is taken from his obituary in the *British Medical Journal*. It said:

> Dr Harry Graham Davies OBE LRCP MRCS, formerly a general practitioner in Llanidloes, Powys, died aged 91. He qualified in medicine at Guy's Hospital in 1925. He was born in Llanelli and his first experience of general practice was in Tredegar, in the same practice where A J Cronin had worked. He played rugby for Wales, getting two Welsh caps as a centre, and was a firm supporter of the Tredegar Medical Practice and later the NHS. He was the complete family doctor and an accomplished *accoucheur*, unaffected by rotas and answering services. His rural practice was vast, and coverage made possible by his use of fast driven sports cars. The cottage hospital "belonged" to the general practitioners. He enthused over driving, and sporadically over golf and sailing. Graham never looked old, and his bald head popping around a bedroom door was therapeutic. His wife Joey, a Guy's nurse, and their children Ann (a nurse) and John (a GP) were an integral part of his life as a GP in rural Wales.

Tredegar Medical Aid Society

Graham Davies played rugby for Guy's and Llanelli, and for Wales against Ireland and France. The game against Ireland was played during 'the troubles', when the Irish people fought for an independent state separate from the rest of the UK, and when this aim was achieved fought a civil war between themselves. The match was held in Belfast when the atmosphere in the country was so uncertain that British soldiers lined the stadium, and faced the spectators with their rifles at the port – across the chest – ready for any emergency. After qualifying, Graham worked at the Royal Gwent Hospital in Newport, then applied for a post as a GP with the Tredegar Medical Aid Society. This was a plum job in the Valleys, given only to the best – though it did help to have played rugby for Wales. His predecessor was A J Cronin, who left the practice for Harley Street and became famous as author of *The Citadel*, a novel based on his experiences among the Welsh miners. Cronin was a good physician but not, Graham said, a particularly good surgeon. As part of the package, Graham was given as his home in Tredegar a house called The Glen, the house that Cronin had occupied before him. The Tredegar practice was innovatory, and it was unique in providing the community with a health care system that became the pattern for the National Health Service when this was established in 1948. The system was simple. For a small weekly donation taken from their wages, local people were entitled to free medical help when it was required. This included medicines, spectacles, any appliances they needed and free referral to other centres when necessary. A wage earner's family and pensioners were included in the scheme. The society employed a team of five doctors, two dentists, three dispensers, a nurse and supporting staff. The central figure was a surgeon, Dr Edwin Davies, who was appointed Chief Medical Officer, and Medical Superintendent of the cottage hospital, in 1914. He retired in 1948. Graham always spoke highly of him and regarded him as one of the best surgeons in the country.

Although primarily a GP, Graham was also the anaesthetist (open chloroform or ether) for Edwin Davies, and the local Medical Officer of Health. Sometimes he spoke of his experiences at Tredegar. One story he related was of a child he saw with pneumonia in the town. Antibiotics were not available and there was no effective treatment that could be given to help the boy to fight the infection. But Graham always kept up to date with the medical journals and, having read of a new treatment that might be effective against pneumonia, he prescribed it. The child survived and Graham said to the mother later, "Mrs Jones didn't that medicine I gave you for Gwyn work well?" She replied, "Doctor, I didn't give it to him. When you told me that Gwyn had pneumonia, I told Harry to go up to the hills and bring me a sheep skin. He did what I asked and we wrapped Gwyn in the skin and that's what cured him." Graham also spoke of country folk putting bread in the rafters and placing the mouldy bits on wounds to heal infections.

More will be said about Graham later, but I will just add this here. He was a modest and generous man. He had no private patients after the inception of the NHS, nor did any of his partners. In Llanidloes he had many rich patients, among them Miss Margaret and Miss Gwendoline Davies of Gregynog. These two sisters were well-known patrons of the arts, and their bequests include a priceless collection of French Impressionist paintings and sculpture that can be seen in the City of Cardiff Art Gallery. Incidentally, when I last went to see the Miss Davieses bequest in Cardiff, it was on loan in the USA. They also left their home, Gregynog Hall, with 700 acres of land, to the University of Wales. The hall is used for various academic purposes but is also the centre for the Institute of Rural Health. Graham cared for these two ladies for over forty years, and he used to visit them every Tuesday afternoon for tea and chat. He also looked after their brother, Lord Davies of Llandinam, and various nephews and nieces. Lord Davies was his patient in the 1940s and, when he was dying of lung cancer, Graham would visit him at Plas Dinam, his home, each week to aspirate his chest so he could breathe more easily.

Graham responded to every request for help and turned no one down. Mary, the matron of Llanidloes hospital, phoned one night as she wanted me to see a man in casualty with a painful arm. I went to find the patient in great pain, with a haemarthrosis of the elbow. I could have given him some analgesic tablets but knew that the quickest way to relieve the pain would be to aspirate the blood from the joint. This I had not seen done, though aspirating knees was fairly commonplace for us. I therefore telephoned Graham and asked him to come and oversee the process to make sure it was done properly. His voice sounded unusually feeble but he said yes and came to the hospital to supervise my aspiration of the elbow. Then he left. Mary told me that she had contacted him first but he had asked her to get me instead, as he was not well and had gone to bed. By that time he was probably in his early seventies.

Obstetrics in mid Wales

Graham's remarkable expertise as an obstetrician was mentioned in his obituary, and I saw him deliver a baby at Llanidloes Hospital using a method that few consultant obstetricians will have seen: an internal version for a deep transverse arrest, followed by a breech delivery. The mother was in labour with her first baby, but her contractions were no longer able to expel the child along the birth passage. She needed help. A Caesarean Section would be the most appropriate procedure nowadays but it was not an option then, we were thirty miles from the nearest obstetric unit, so a mid-cavity forceps delivery was agreed by the midwife and doctors. Tom Brittain anaesthetised the mother with chloroform and Graham applied axis traction forceps without difficulty but the baby was so tightly wedged that he could not extract the infant. The situation had reached crisis point so Graham removed the forceps and did an internal version. In other words, he pushed the baby back into the uterus, turned it around within the womb, pulled the legs down and delivered the child feet first as a breech. It was masterful. Both mother and child did well. Few obstetricians in the UK will have attempted such a manoeuvre and then only if they were working in a Third World country. But the way Graham did it, it looked so easy, even though he was under great stress. He used to say that in the 1920s, when he started practicing obstetrics, the infant and maternal mortality rates were so high that the primary aim was to finish with a live mother. If you had a live baby as well, that was a bonus.

After I had joined the practice, mothers used to ask me if they could have the baby at home. I always said no, and promised that if they had the baby in the cottage hospital they could be home in 48 hours. Then they would go to see Graham and he would say yes. But sometimes Graham was disabled with lumbago or migraine and could not attend the birth. Then, when the delivery was imminent, the midwife would phone me and I would collect Graham's obstetric bag and go to the house, to be present at the birth, though rarely to deliver the baby. These home deliveries were easy and uneventful, but there was always the uncertainty that something might go suddenly wrong. Graham used to say that, when he retired, he would miss home deliveries most, because they were such happy occasions. I was surprised when I learnt that home childbirth was his greatest delight; he had such expertise in dealing with accidents and trauma that I thought he would miss those most of all. But clearly I was wrong.

There was one birth I regretted not attending. The parents lived in a pantechnicon, a converted furniture van, which I first visited when their infant son was feverish and miserable. It was a stormy day and I remember the father, dressed only in shirt and jeans, running through heavy rain to open gates in the fields for me to pass through. The child had a middle ear infection and responded quickly to the penicillin that I prescribed for otitis media in those days. On a later visit I had a better chance to assess their living quarters. Their bed was made of wood and was fixed to the front of the van's interior, high behind the driver's cab. The other furnishings were simple. A cushioned bench extended along one side, while the facing wall was lined with books. There were works on alchemy, mysticism, philosophy and two that I had read

– *The Tibetan Book of the Dead* and *The I Ching*. Photographs and a tantric painting were fixed on a wall above the couch, and a stove stood near the door at the back of the van. *The Tibetan Book of the Dead* and *The I Ching* proved a talking point and we discovered a common interest in the writings of Carl Jung. The man was much more widely read in Jung's books than any medical doctor of my acquaintance and he introduced me to Jung's thoughts on synchronicity. We talked at length as this was my first opportunity to discuss Jung with someone conversant with his works. The setting was unusual: seated in a pantechnicon with a naked baby in a wicker basket nearby and fields visible outside is not the customary place for the writings of a famous psychiatrist to be discussed, but it was the way it happened. Both parents had known affluence but had chosen a simpler mode of life. They had travelled widely and were planning a trip to India where they hoped to meet the Dalai Lama. Before going abroad, they moved the van to Staylittle, a hamlet in the hills even further from Llanidloes. There their second baby was born. They wanted me to attend the birth but I persisted in my determination that the child should be delivered in the hospital and was not present. They had the baby in the pantechnicon and I was not there. Olwen Hamer, the midwife, said it was a lovely birth.

Graham Davies at Llanidloes

Graham moved to Llanidloes in the 1930s. This should not be considered as an escape from the harsh reality of industrial life to the soft ways of the country. The hill farmers, who were to be his patients had medical problems that were not seen by GPs in large towns or even in the mining villages of south Wales, and the Welsh rural communities also had their full share of the social problems of the age. Whilst many lived in well-equipped homes, the most isolated dwelt in houses with no indoor sanitation or running water. The living conditions of some were so dreadful that I found them comparable with the huts of the Inuit in Labrador, filthy hovels with no facilities. I remember visiting a lovely couple aged ninety, whose drinking water came from a pipe jutting from the hillside 100 yards from their house. That was in the 1960s. They said it was the best water in the area, it was certainly the coldest I had drunk. They were fortunate in being well cared for by a young man called Alfred, who had known them for many years. There were fairly affluent farmers in and around Llanidloes but the healthy, rubicund farmer depicted in paintings and novels was often a caricature of the reality living on the Welsh hill farms. Farmer's Lung, an allergic response to fungal spores that grow in wet hay, was common, mainly because in the rain-swept hills the hay was damp, and could not be adequately dried, and also because the corticosteroids that are effective in the early stages of the disease were not widely used then. Most doctors in the UK knew nothing about the disease, though it disabled as readily as the pneumoconiosis which damaged the lungs of coal miners, which was more widely publicised. Other hazards which were specific to the rural community in my time included fatal farm accidents, brucellosis and a high suicide rate.

When Graham moved into Llanidloes, he had to compete for patients as there were two medical practices in the town. One was headed by Walter Davies, whom Graham joined; the other by Dr Vaughan, and later by his partner Dr Lee Shimmin. Graham would have nothing to do with the other practice until Dr Shimmin retired in 1962 and his younger partner, Dr Tudor Howell, joined us. This was essentially a business arrangement but it united the practices and enabled each of us to have half a day a week free and alternate weekends off. It also enabled me to establish a research area, in which the residents were all patients of the practice. Within this well-defined area, I undertook two studies on bereavement which will be discussed later. Both are still quoted. I never met Dr Vaughan, though his son, a history teacher, returned to the town when he retired and, like his father, was well liked. My contact with Dr Shimmin was slight but his patients spoke highly of him and he was probably a more reflective person than Graham. I believe his son became an ENT consultant in Cardiff. Like myself, Tudor Howell trained at St Thomas's Hospital, London. He was older than I and we never met as students but my wife was friendly with his sister at Howells School, Cardiff, and had stayed at their home near Neath. Tudor had his own purpose-built surgery at Caersws, on the periphery of our united practice, and pursued an independent role though he became, in effect, the practice manager. He became head of the St John Ambulance Brigade in Montgomeryshire and High Sheriff of the County. His wife Sally, who had trained as a nurse at St Thomas's, was also an active and senior member of the Ambulance Brigade.

Like Dr John Hunt in London, Graham's partner, Walter Davies, visited his patients in a chauffeur driven car. Walter's wife kept the practice accounts and sent the bills to his patients. If any complained of being overcharged, Walter would disclaim any responsibility, saying he had no control over his wife. He invited consultants from London and Liverpool to visit Llanidloes, and they saw patients in Abernant and in the cottage hospital after it was opened in 1930. A surgeon from Aberystwyth came when needed, visiting patients in their homes and operating on their kitchen tables. He was well known as an excellent surgeon with a charismatic personality. He had won a half blue at Oxford for billiards, and I knew a GP-anaesthetist in Caerphilly who decided to become a doctor when this surgeon, whose name escapes me, removed his brother's inflamed appendix at their home in Llandinam. If the journey home to Aberystwyth was at night, the surgeon and his driver would stop at the George Borrow Inn in Ponterwyd, and share a bottle of whisky that the landlord had waiting for them. Life was possibly lighter hearted for motorists and doctors then, and Walter was a regular member of the shooting parties that Captain Crawshay, a prominent sportsman and industrialist, arranged in the district, lodging his guests at the Lion Hotel at Llandinam. The Lion was a temperance hotel at the time and not licensed to sell alcohol, but this legality was easily circumvented by Captain Crawshay. He simply told his batman to bring into the hotel all the alcohol that would be required by his guests. I have a fond memory of that inn. The landlady's daughter was expecting her first child and had arranged with Graham for the baby to be delivered at home. On the night of the birth, Graham was not available and the midwife summoned me. I arrived just before the baby was born, expecting the midwife to deliver the child but she asked me to do so, possibly because the woman's mother was present. It was an easy birth with the baby's new grandmother sitting by the bed.

Walter's son and daughter visited Abernant during my residence there. The daughter came to see the daffodils and roses she had planted in the front garden, the son to visit the house. He knocked on the door one day and announced: "I am Billy Davies, I used to live here, can I have a look around?" The name was familiar, so I said yes and showed him around the house. When we reached the bedroom I shared with my wife, he looked inside and said, "This is where my father delivered my mother of me". Billy died sometime after visiting Llanidloes and I was surprised but pleased to see that he had a full obituary in *The Times* written by his friend Erskine Childers, son of the Irish Republican leader and author of the same name. From the obituary I learnt that Billy was well known in Canada for his work among the Inuit as a doctor in the North West Territories. It is remarkable that two doctors associated with Abernant, and having no other connection to each other, should have worked with the Canadian Inuit, one in the North West Territories, the other (myself) in the north-east of Canada. Carl Jung might have regarded this coincidence as an example of synchronicity, which he defined as two unrelated events that had a meaningful association. The founder of Gordonstoun School, Kurt Hahn, was quite a regular visitor to Abernant. This was during World War II, when Gordonstoun School was evacuated from Scotland to Llandinam, and Graham Davies was the school doctor. He told me that Kurt Hahn enjoyed walking in the garden at Abernant, usually meditatively, with bowed head and hands clasped behind his back, in a manner that his pupil, Prince Phillip, also favoured. I had no connection with the school but was intrigued as I had spent most of my military service at Elgin, the town most closely located to Gordonstoun, and just 15 minutes from the school by car.

Graham spoke sometimes of the stories that Walter Davies narrated, and it is obvious that his partner had not only a wealth of knowledge but a wicked sense of humour, as the following account indicates. A woman came to Walter complaining of being troubled by a witch and he resolved the problem immediately. I am not sure if the treatment he arranged took place in Abernant or at the woman's home, but he placed a table in the centre of a room and put a candlestick on top of the table. Then he lit the candle and told the woman to undress. After she had done so, he told her to run around the table saying "go away witch, go away witch, go away witch". The time she spent running around the table is not known, nor which clothes she removed, but this unconventional treatment cured her, and she never complained of being troubled by a witch again. No doctor would dare to do anything similar today, but I doubt if present remedies would be so quickly effective. Also, I wonder if Walter's method was so unusual in those days. In the early twentieth century, considerable respect was given to folk healers in mid Wales, though they were sometimes condemned by church leaders. The Rev. Dr Martyn Lloyd-Jones was the most prominent of their critics, having been a consultant at St Bartholomew's Hospital and a Harley

Street physician before being ordained in the Calvinistic Methodist Church. His first ministerial post was at Aberavon in 1927. More will be said about these traditional healers, who were known in mid Wales as conjurors, later in this section.

The Llanidloes Practice

When Graham joined Walter Davies in Llanidloes he moved into the heart of Wales and into one of the oldest boroughs in the Principality. His new home was located in the first town on the River Severn (*Hafren* in Welsh), a town famous for its timber-framed buildings, and for the independent spirit of its citizens. It had received a charter to hold a market in 1289 but had existed for at least 400 years before that date. At one time the surrounding area was an important centre for mining silver and lead, and the town itself once had a thriving flannel industry. But by the 1930s the main source of income for the farmers came from rearing sheep, whilst light industries and a foundry provided work for people within the town. The practice area was extensive. It was larger than the metropolitan police area of London, extending from Rhayader to Newtown, from Abbey Cwm Hir (with its ruined Cistercian abbey) to the remote village of Staylittle, and across Pumlumon Mountain to Eisteddfa Gurig. The villages and hamlets within its boundaries included Llangurig, Llandinam, Llawr-y-glyn, Cwmbelan, Caersws, Carno, Pant-y-dŵr, Trefeglwys and Saint Harmon's. Welsh was commonly spoken in the upland areas and, though not a requirement, it helped that Graham was bilingual, as was another partner Tudor Howell. The area was beautiful but access to homesteads could be difficult, particularly in the winter, when snow might block the roads and tracks for days, even weeks. The River Wye and the River Severn both had their source in Pumlumon and flowed through the area towards the sea.

Graham settled in Castle House, a Grade II listed building in the centre of the town. He saw patients there whilst Walter continued to practice from his surgery in Abernant. Theirs was a dispensing practice; red tablets being prescribed for anaemia, green tablets for anxiety, white tablets for pain or as sedatives. Bottles of medicine were made up from Winchesters, large, narrow-necked bottles containing concentrates of the medicine. An appropriate amount of the concentrate was placed in a 'medicine' bottle, topped up with water, sealed with a cork and given to the patient. *Mist Morph et Ipecac* was a popular cough medicine and *Mist Brom et Valerian* was often prescribed for depression, possibly because it tasted horrible. These medicines were still requested by patients when I joined the practice, and the system was common in pharmacies throughout the country. Dispensing was less easy then than now. All tablets had to be counted. There were no pre-packed tablets, and few medicines were available in pre-packed bottles. Abernant and Castle House each had a dispenser, Miss Parry and Marjorie, and both also acted as the receptionist. They were local ladies who knew everyone and were very efficient. They handled telephone calls, patients' records, medicines and the patients themselves. They were always cheerful and never complained. Medicines were dispensed when requested and no patient was expected to give prior notice of their needs, or wait 48 hours before they could collect their prescriptions. It was an efficient system.

Abernant and Castle House were lovely residences, with well-proportioned surgeries, waiting rooms and dispensaries. Castle House had a well in its cellar and older patients liked their medicine to be dispensed with water from its well. Others preferred water from the White House, a nearby house where the dentist lived and practised. Graham decided to test the purity of the two sources of water and sent samples of water from both wells to be analysed. The results were interesting. No fault was found with the water from Castle House, but the White House water was declared unfit for human consumption. This happened in the 1930s and I wondered why they used water from the wells when both houses had water on tap. It seems that established preferences take a long time to disappear.

The Cottage Hospital

Llanidloes War Memorial Hospital was important to the community and the doctors. Graham spent a lot of time there and its newest ward is named after him. This was no more than he deserved as he supported the hospital in many ways, both in service to the staff and patients, and financially. The cottage hospital enabled us to care for our patients within an 18-bedded unit, meet the consultants on their regular visits from Aberystwyth, and have direct access to physiotherapy, X-ray and pathology services. We also had a 30-bed geriatric unit that Graham had been instrumental in establishing. It was separate from the main building but was run entirely by the GPs until a consultant geriatrician was appointed in the 1970s. Few areas in the UK provided such excellent facilities for the local community and its doctors, with minimal cost to the NHS. Phyllis Carruthers, the hospital matron and her nurses were very efficient and supportive. They gave our patients injections when we asked, took bloods for us, and provided a chaperone service when we needed it for gynaecological and post-natal examinations. Some were local girls who had trained elsewhere and returned to Llanidloes. Mary Jones, who trained in London and became matron later, was one such returnee. We could always rely on them and, I think, they on us. Since the 1960s, administrators in the Health Service have sought periodically to close the hospital; this was discussed when I was in Llanidloes but it was fiercely contested by the local community then, and continues to be resisted now. But changes are inevitable and GPs no longer work the hours they used to do. That is understandable as we allowed ourselves to be overworked, but the maternity unit closed after I left and babies are no longer delivered in Llanidloes Hospital. Instead, mothers travel to units elsewhere, such as Newtown, where their own doctors can no longer attend the births.

The consultant service provided by doctors from Bronglais Hospital in Aberystwyth was better than any I have encountered since. No patient waited more than a few days to see a general surgeon or physician. Maternity and gynaecological cases were seen within a fortnight, and patients with ophthalmic or orthopaedic problems were also seen within two weeks. The chest physician based at Machynlleth came once a month and provided an excellent service to an area where Farmers Lung was widespread. Local GPs were welcomed at these clinics and Graham was always present when his patients were seen. Not every local practitioner was able to attend the clinics as frequently but they were always welcomed, and patients generally liked their doctor to be present at the consultations. I overheard one lady saying to a friend: "My doctor was not there to stand over me," when she saw the specialist. Graham had a particularly close relationship with the consultants and he used these meetings to keep up to date with current medical trends. He was knowledgeable and practical, and helped with routine tasks in the hospital. In his seventies he took on the task of giving intra-articular injections to the finger joints for the visiting orthopaedic surgeon.

World War II

When World War II broke out, Graham wanted to join the army. Age-wise he was probably a borderline candidate for military service but Walter Davies vetoed any move. He threatened to retire if Graham enlisted, leaving the area short of doctors. So Graham stayed in Llanidloes throughout the war and moved into Abernant when Walter retired. There was little military activity in that quiet area of Wales but a platoon of the Home Guard was formed locally, and a Spitfire crashed in nearby Cwmbelan. Graham was called to the accident and arrived to find the plane lying in the stream that flowed through the village. Little damage was done to the buildings in the village but the plane was smashed and the pilot badly injured. He could not extract himself from the plane, but Graham and local men managed to ease him out of the cockpit and place him on the ground. Then, to move him safely, Graham took a bed from one of the cottages and commandeered a local lorry. With the man lying on the bed and the bed on the lorry, he accompanied the pilot to the cottage hospital and treated him as best he could, but sadly the man died despite this care. Graham was used to dealing with accidents and serious injuries, and was as effective as any doctor could be in the circumstances, but he said that the pilot's mother never forgave him for the way he had treated her son. She was most upset by his decision to convey the injured man to hospital on a truck and not, as she considered proper, by ambulance.

A less serious, but more bizarre injury, confronted Graham when he returned from a fishing trip in Cardigan Bay. A man had been admitted to the cottage hospital having deliberately injured himself. In a moment of religious fervour the man had cut off his own penis, literally responding to the biblical injunction "if your member offends you cut it off". Bleeding was not excessive but there was a gap that needed to be closed which Graham did by stitching part of the scrotum over the denuded area. After the wound was closed, the man was transferred to the psychiatric hospital at Talgarth, near Brecon. He remained there for a long time.

Gordonstoun School at Llandinam

The wartime association between mid Wales and Gordonstoun School is not well known, but during World War II Gordonstoun School was required to leave its site in Scotland and move elsewhere. National security was the primary reason for the school's relocation. Its position close to the Moray Firth, and to the nearby air stations of Lossiemouth and Kinross, was regarded as highly sensitive by naval intelligence, particularly as Kurt Hahn, the school's headmaster and founder, was a German by birth and had served in the German Department of Foreign Affairs during World War I. In 1933, then headmaster of Salem School in southern Germany, he spoke against the Nazi party and was imprisoned by Hitler, who only released him following a direct appeal from the British Prime Minister, Ramsey MacDonald. Hitler allowed Hahn to leave Germany and come to Britain, where he was offered the headship of Eton College, but he chose instead to settle in Scotland and establish Gordonstoun School by the sea, in Morayshire.

When the school had to be relocated for the duration of the war, Lord Davies of Llandinam, brother to the Miss Davieses of Gregynog Hall, who have been mentioned already, offered a house named Broneirion to the school. The offer was accepted and the school moved to Llandinam, which is a lovely village (population 350) on the River Severn just a few miles from Llanidloes. A statue of its most famous son, the nineteenth-century entrepreneur, David Davies, stands in a prominent position within the village, whilst a replica of this statue stands in my home town of Barry, as David Davies built Barry Docks, which became the most important coal exporting port in the world. Also, in 1864, he built Broneirion as a home for his family, and it was this beautiful house, with its splendid location in the Severn Vale that his grandson Lord Davies offered as a temporary residence to Gordonstoun School. The school remained there throughout World War II and Graham Davies became the school doctor.

When the war ended Hahn helped Prince Phillip to set up the Duke of Edinburgh Award scheme. He was also the motivating force in establishing the Outward Bound Schools and the United World Colleges. The first of these international colleges was established at St Donat's in south Wales and Rhydian Brittain, a son of my partner Tom Brittain, was among the first students to enter the college when it opened in 1961. Graham, who was a great admirer of Kurt Hahn, told me of an outbreak of measles that occurred in the school when he was its doctor. One boy was ill but had no specific sign of measles except for a single Koplik Spot that Graham had seen in the mouth. These small red spots, with a white centre like a grain of salt, appear on the mucous membranes of the mouth early in the disease and are diagnostic, so Graham informed the headmaster who told the parents that the boy had measles. When no rash appeared Graham began to doubt his diagnosis, having seen only one Koplik Spot when usually more can be seen, and was greatly relieved when the rash appeared several days later. Throughout this uncertain period he felt completely supported by Hahn.

Childhood Diseases

Outbreaks of measles, and other infectious diseases, were common among children in the 1960s, but the pattern has changed dramatically since then. This, of course, is due to the widespread use of immunisation to prevent these diseases developing, but when the government decided that children should be immunised against measles, I found myself in a conundrum. David, my youngest child, had not been infected with measles and I would have preferred him to obtain the natural immunity conferred by the disease than to be an early recipient of this new vaccine. But I gave him

the injection because I knew I could not advise other parents
to have their children immunised if I had not immunised
my own son. The need to immunise against infectious
diseases confronted me daily, in fact whenever I saw Miss
Parry my receptionist. She was a very able lady whose life
had been blighted in childhood by poliomyelitis, and for
the remainder of her life she needed to wear a calliper. I
remembered also my own experience of infectious diseases
when I was a child. Our family doctor came to see me on
two occasions only, and both times he sent me to the fever
hospital, first aged four with scarlet fever, then aged eight
with diphtheria. During those stays in hospital I never saw
my parents, for though they used to visit they were not
allowed on the ward. They could look at me through the
window, but I could not see them as they were required
to conceal their faces from me in case I became upset at
not being able to join them, which they did by holding
brown paper, pierced with eye-holes in front of their faces.
Thanks to immunisation, I only saw one other person with
diphtheria and that was in Labrador.

Every winter there were the usual outbreaks of flu, and
also on one occasion a local Hepatitis A epidemic. Many
children were infected by the Hepatitis virus and the requests
for home visits naturally escalated as the mothers wanted
the diagnosis to be confirmed, and to be reassured that the
care they were giving was appropriate. Among adolescents,
glandular fever was common and had to be distinguished
from other throat infections, but was readily diagnosed by
sending blood to the laboratory. We used the Paul-Bunnell
test but I believe the Monospot test is more commonly used
these days. Two teenage girls were more severely affected
than most and of these one later developed schizophrenia,
though whether the glandular fever was a precipitating
factor is doubtful.

Although chicken pox is usually a mild disease in

childhood, it is more troublesome in adults and, later in life, can reappear as shingles. Because of the associated pain, herpes zoster was a disease I never liked seeing in elderly people, and I was surprised to read recently in a medical textbook that the pain it causes is usually mild and transient. That was not my experience, but the modern use of antiviral drugs early in the disease may have transformed the situation from that experienced in the past.

Involvement with the College of GPs

As a student, I was told that the best general practitioners worked in remote areas and far from the teaching hospitals. That assessment may not be true now, but it was certainly true when I joined Graham in 1960, and I knew then that I was a fortunate person to have joined him in Llanidloes. I should not eulogize Graham but, except for Tony Paddon in Labrador, I know no one comparable to him then or now, and I was acquainted with some of the best-known people in general practice in those early days. Soon after the College of General Practitioners was founded, I became an associate of the college and was elected a Fellow in 1972. I served on the faculty board and research committee of the south Wales faculty of the college, and when this was split joined the south-west Wales faculty board and research committee. Graham was invited to be a founder member of the college but declined the invitation. He was a hands-on doctor, and too involved with patient care to be interested in joining a new college that was being established by mainly city doctors. Nor were my other partners interested in the college when I arrived, though Tudor Howell did become an MRCGP and a college trainer. Meanwhile, both Tudor and Tom Brittain were closely involved with the local medical committee, Tudor as secretary and Tom as its chairman.

A Fortunate Man

John Sassall was probably the most iconic English country doctor in the 1960s. He was a single-handed practitioner who lived in the Forest of Dean, and exemplified what many thought was best about general practice in the postwar period. He was not well known to his peers, but his life and work was brought to general notice by John Berger (author) and Jean Mohr (photographer) in their book *A Fortunate Man*.[10] In it they portrayed Sassall's life as a doctor with a fascinating mosaic of words and pictures, and I was fortunate enough to be asked to review it for the *British Medical Journal*. In it I saw much of my own life and practice as a country doctor, both its ups and downs, but I was not as isolated as Sassell and had colleagues who were supportive. The book was entitled *A Fortunate Man*, not because Sassall was particularly talented or lucky, but because he dealt with the essentials of life, and worked in close harmony with his patients and the environment in which they lived. All this has changed. General practitioners are much less likely now to be greatly involved with people's really significant moments in life – their birth and death. Nor do they visit people at home very often, yet a faded photograph somewhere in the house can suddenly provide a new insight into the life of the old person they have come to see. John Sassall had this close relationship with people over many years. So did Graham Davies and my other partners. But they were not always good moments. There was grief and failure, and a feature of Berger's book are the moments of deep depression that Dr John Sassall experienced. He was a lonely man and after his wife died he committed suicide.

Around this time the *British Medical Journal* asked about twenty of us to write a regular 'Personal View' of about 1,000 words, focussing on a topic from our experience in medical practice that might be related to friends at dinner. I contributed for a few years. The journal gave these personal views no individual title but it did give titles to a number of personal views that it published as an anthology in 1975. The one they published which was written by me was given the title 'A Fortunate Man'[11] which I found both surprising and apt. Thinking back, it reminds me of a letter that Graham had received from a friend and senior consultant in London. He showed me the letter and in it his friend had written 'How fortunate are the doctors who live in Llandinam'.

Rural Accidents

The catchment area at Llanidloes was vast and hilly. Much of it was designated as an area of special difficulty for rural practice mileage payments, and it was our custom to attend all road and tractor accidents in the locality. At that time the ambulance service in the county of Montgomery was unique. It was manned entirely by volunteers, mostly by men engaged in full-time employment. All were members of the St John Ambulance Brigade and they received their medical training within the community. Dr Graham Davies OStJ (Officer of St John) was the surgeon for the Llanidloes division, whilst I became the surgeon for the division based at Llangurig. There were no paramedics and no helicopter ambulance service. A call to an accident took precedence over whatever else the ambulance men or doctors might be doing, and local employers recognised this as important. Elsewhere in the UK, particularly in the more remote and inaccessible regions, other enthusiastic GPs provided similar services. One practitioner, whose name is lost in time, provided the first such service to casualties on the M1 in Yorkshire, whilst doctors in Rugby equipped and trained themselves for similar work in their area. The Rugby doctors carried radio-telephones in their cars, though we found that was impractical within the hills of mid Wales. Yet the medical press scarcely mentioned this work, nor did it report on the problems confronting the doctors and the casualties in these difficult situations. Nothing, for instance, had been published by the late 1960s on the injuries sustained in agricultural tractor accidents, and little on the management of casualties in transit to hospital. As I became increasingly aware of the fatal injuries caused by tractor accidents, and of the work done at road traffic accidents by people like Graham, I decided to look at the problems more closely.

Tractor Accidents

My first experience of a tractor accident has been mentioned already in this book. I was a house surgeon on the obstetric unit of the Caerphilly and District Miners' Hospital and responded to a police request for a doctor to attend an accident outside the town. I did not expect the scene that confronted us. A tractor was overturned on the hillside, a dead man lay nearby and rooks pecked at his scattered brains. Five years later I attended my next accident. The scene had changed, to a more rural part of Wales. I had completed my first morning surgery at Abernant and had driven to Caersws, where a second surgery was held in the sitting room of Glenys Parsons' house. Glenys was lovely, a slender woman who had married a huge Cockney, Jack Parsons, whose elderly father later married Glenys's widowed mother. Glenys had one daughter and they all seemed happy together. Everyone was welcome in the house and a cup of tea was always ready for visitors including me. One day I had finished the surgery when the telephone rang. It was Miss Parry, my receptionist. She had received an urgent call from a farm in the hills, and I was wanted immediately to attend a tractor accident. I was not best pleased, in fact I was annoyed because I had so much more work to do. I was expected at Llandinam Post Office and then at the hospital and the pressure was mounting. I left immediately and drove into the hills, only to find the injured man sitting in the farmhouse smiling at me. Luckily

I held my anger and listened to his story. He was a man in his early twenties who had taken a tractor on to the hills, and was on a slope when the tractor slipped and rolled down the hill. He did not jump off, but stayed on until it overturned and left him lying on the ground, while it continued to roll into the valley. I believe the young man made his own way back home. He was enormously lucky because the tractor could easily have crushed and killed him. Providence had helped in the form of a dip. When the tractor overturned, it did so over a cavity in the hill, which gave the driver enough protection for him not to be crushed. He got away with a few squashed vertebrae, and fortunately was not severely injured as the fractures were not caused by the direct weight of the tractor on his spine. After that incident, I never grumbled about going to a tractor accident. I was just happy if the driver survived and was not injured.

Two other tractor accidents are worth mentioning. A farmer's son was driving his tractor on a high hill. The ground was wet and slippery and he had attached Davril strakes to the wheels to provide greater stability, but the tractor slipped, turned over and crushed him before rolling all the way down the hill. He was thrown off the tractor and found lying injured, unable to walk. A door was removed from a house or barn, and he was placed on it and carried to the farmhouse. I was summoned and found him badly injured, in pain and bleeding from the urethra. I gave him an injection of pethidine, and he was taken by ambulance to Bronglais Hospital in Aberystwyth where a ruptured prostatic urethra was repaired. He made a full recovery and returned to work 20 weeks later. I saw his father in the surgery and asked him to put a safety cab on the tractor, now that his son had been injured. He said it wasn't necessary, repeating the view expressed to Welsh farmers by Cledwyn Hughes MP, later Minister for Agriculture, Fisheries and Food. At the time Hughes was saying that tractors were safe and the problem was with the drivers, not the vehicle. Later the same farmer whose son had been injured drove a tractor that overturned, and was crushed and killed by it.

Another incident involved a man whose tractor overturned on the hills early one morning. It did not skid down a slope but fell on flat land, where the soil was soft and marshy. The alarm was not raised until late that evening when he failed to return home. A search party went to find him and found him lying under the tractor, pinned to the ground by a wheel that held his arm and shoulder firmly stuck in the soft soil. He had lain there for about twelve hours and, in his desperation, had tried to kill himself with a penknife. He was released and taken by ambulance to Bronglais Hospital where he went into renal failure and almost died. He survived but with a permanently damaged arm. In July 1965, the *British Medical Journal* published a paper I wrote on Agricultural Tractor Accidents.[12] It was the first report to deal specifically with tractor accidents in an English-language journal and provided details of fourteen accidents. It reached the following conclusions:

1. If a driver is injured when a tractor overturns, the chances are about 1 in 4 that he will be killed.

2. Tractor accidents have a much higher mortality and serious injury rate than road traffic accidents.

3. Tractor accidents produce injuries of the crush type, and the trunk is more likely to be injured than the head or extremities.

4. The man most likely to be involved in a tractor accident is one who is married, is an experienced driver and is over 30 years old.

5. Tractors should be provided with safety frames that are strong enough to protect drivers from being crushed if the vehicle overturns.

I cannot claim that the article had any influence on public policy, but I do know that the UK Parliament passed a Bill in 1967 requiring all new agricultural tractors to be fitted with a safety cab when first sold to the farmer or used by a worker after 1st September 1970. Later, in November 1973, the Parliamentary Secretary to the Ministry of Agriculture, Fisheries and Food (Mrs Penny Fisher) informed Parliament that deaths from overturning tractors in the UK was the lowest on record.[13]

Road Traffic Accidents (RTAs)

When I was in Llanidloes, people expected their GPs to be available in moments of crisis and to go to road traffic accidents. If the call came during a busy surgery, we would inform any patients in the waiting room and leave immediately. Some patients would stay, others would return later. There was never any dissent, the next crisis might be a call to a member of their family. We could not have provided that service if we had an appointment system. When the call came, the ambulance drivers, doctors and police would hurry to the scene of accident, always hoping to find no one injured. The police were usually the last to arrive, probably because they had the furthest to travel. Initially, I was not experienced in accident trauma and learnt a lot from St John Ambulance men, especially Granville Morgan, an engine driver, and PC Price, a police constable who was based at Llangurig. Some accidents were gory and eventually I could not travel around the practice area without passing places where someone had been killed or severely injured. At a bridge near Cwmbelan, three young Irish men died from multiple injuries when their car crashed into the stone bridge. Nearer Llanidloes, two local teenagers were killed when a lad from the town smashed into their motorbikes whilst he was driving down a steep hill. It was an accident, he had obviously not seen them, but a real disaster for the community. On that occasion, Police Sergeant Davies sent me to comfort the mother of one of the dead boys – she was beyond consolation. She already knew of the death when I arrived, so I did not have to inform her, which was a relief. On another occasion, a farmer asked me to go with him to a field to look for his brother, who was missing. We went and found the brother crushed beneath a tractor. Then, we went to the brother's house, but on seeing me his widow knew immediately what had happened. The man went into the house to support his sister-in-law, and I left to inform the police and coroner.

My first RTA was on the mountain road to Staylittle, four miles outside Llanidloes. I have no idea who reported the death, but when I reached the accident site, no one was with the man. I found him lying on the roadside close to his motorbike. He was an Italian mechanic, travelling with a team of motorcyclists through the UK, and must have been following the others to be left alone in that way. Whatever the circumstances, the motorbike had skidded on a bend and his head had struck the road. He was not wearing a crash helmet, but wore a leather cap, which retained his broken skull. I could do nothing to help him, merely inform the coroner. In one year, I saw four young boys with head injuries caused by falling off their bicycles. I left one lad with his mother in an isolated house, telling her to contact me if he became drowsy or sick. Like the others, he recovered with no ill effects, but today few doctors would consider a mother to be the most reliable person to care for a child with a head injury. Immediate transfer to hospital with regular observation by nurses would be considered mandatory, in case emergency treatment was required.

In 1968, I published data that I had collected on road traffic accidents within the practice area over a four and a half year period. The information came from various sources, including the ambulance log book, the coroner's records, the police RTA reports, the hospital records and the practice records. The paper provided data on 124 road traffic and tractor accidents in an area of about 110 square miles.[14] Over 200 people were involved, of whom 11 died

(10 at the site and 1 in hospital), and 80 were seriously injured. A further 110 received minor injuries. Graham and I attended 49 accidents, and another doctor attended one. No person died in transit to hospital, though the distances travelled were often great, with patients being sent to hospitals in Aberystwyth, Chepstow, Liverpool, Oswestry, Morriston, Shrewsbury and Wrexham, depending on their need. Burns went to Chepstow, neurological problems to Morriston and children to Wrexham. Our in transit survival data compared favourably with those published by Gissane and Bull from the Birmingham Accident Hospital, though the ambulance service in Birmingham had much closer access to specialist units than we did in mid Wales.[15] Sixty-five of our casualties were transferred by ambulance, 44 by car (often the doctor's car) and 14 by other types of vehicle. A helicopter was summoned from the search and rescue centre in Anglesey just once, to take a man with a fracture-dislocation of the spine to a hospital, in Oswestry, where sadly he died.

An analysis of the work undertaken by the GPs on the day they attended an accident is interesting, as the figures are quite remarkable. Whilst the incidence of RTAs in the UK peaks towards the weekend, Saturday being a market day was also the busiest day of the week for the practice in Llanidloes. Each doctor on duty held at least a morning, afternoon and evening surgery on Saturday, and an extra surgery if he went to Caersws. A doctor who attended an accident travelled between 26 and 40 miles on that day, as well as seeing approximately 80 patients on a Saturday, ten patients on Sunday, and a variable number during the week. They also visited their patients in the hospital.

The biggest pile-up occurred after I had published the paper on RTAs. There was a major accident between Llandinam and Llanidloes with multiple casualties, and it happened at night. Graham was the doctor to be first informed. Some people were severely injured, but he arranged for all those involved to be taken to the cottage hospital. Then he contacted Ian MacFarlane, the orthopaedic surgeon at Aberystwyth, and they decided that the patients would be treated best at Llanidloes and that Mr MacFarlane would bring his orthopaedic team to the cottage hospital. Everyone became involved and we were up all night dealing with the casualties. Happily they all survived, and regained good function of their injured bones. This included a local lad who was not seen when the casualties were collected by the ambulance men. But before leaving the site, Graham checked the damaged vehicles as he always did at RTAs, and found an unconscious man in a car lying beneath another vehicle. With help Graham extracted him, stopped a passing van, placed the man on the floor of the van and accompanied him to hospital. He was the first casualty the orthopaedic team treated. He had fractures of both femurs, a fractured skull and mandible, and had also broken six ribs. It took him many months to make a full recovery, but happily he did so.

A Pregnant Woman Struck by Lightning

Obstetrics is a relatively minor aspect of the work of a modern general practitioner compared with the old country doctor. Graham Davies was a very experienced obstetrician; I was not, but I did the occasional forceps delivery if it was imperative, and we always attended the birth of our patients' babies. In hospital, these were delivered by the matron, at home by the district midwife, but we were there if needed, if only to comfort the mother and give gas and air. Sometimes, the unexpected happened. On one occasion a mother delivered twins attached to a single placenta. One baby was pink, the other white. Luckily, we had an incubator and they were safely transferred to the baby unit at Wrexham for the expert care they required.

A different kind of uncertainty arose in July 1963 when a young woman was struck by lightning. It happened on a storm swept hill and she was sheltering in a sheep-pen with her husband and father-in-law. The married couple stood together under a corrugated metal sheet, which just touched the nape of her neck. Her father-in-law was sheltering beneath another zinc sheet which rested on his shoulders. He was standing on wet soil and wearing hobnailed boots whilst the others wore rubber wellingtons. Suddenly, they were all knocked to the ground by a flash of lightning and, when they regained consciousness, they saw that the lightning had burnt a field of hay and two rows of larch trees. It had also burnt holes into the ground and destroyed the old man's shirt, coat and left boot. After picking themselves up, they walked to the nearest farmhouse and phoned for a doctor. Not surprisingly, Dr Graham Davies arrived and drove them in his car to the cottage hospital where he admitted the older farmer and his daughter-in-law. Graham noted that the man's left foot was cold, cyanotic, pulse-less and anaesthetic to pinprick. She had a headache which lasted for some hours, and also had the fern-leaf burns of lightning on her face, right shoulder and nape of the neck. Exit burns ran transversely across her bottom. These marks disappeared within 24 hours and she was discharged home two days later. Much later the father gave me his damaged boot, which I kept as a souvenir for many years. A few days after leaving hospital, the woman came to see me complaining of nausea. She was anxious, and slightly agitated, and it transpired that she was pregnant. I reassured her that the lightning strike would not affect her baby and gave her a small dose of barbiturate to take at night and twice daily. The pregnancy proceeded satisfactorily and her anxiety decreased as it progressed. She went into labour naturally and a baby girl was delivered in the hospital by matron just one day before the expected delivery date, weighing in at a healthy 5lbs 10oz (2.55 kg). Her pregnancy and the lightning strike had one unusual feature; it was the first published case of a woman who, having been struck by lightning early in pregnancy, continued with a normal pregnancy to term and then gave birth to a normal infant.

My account of the incident, which was reported in the *British Medical Journal* in 1965,[16] attracted a lot of interest and the family had many presents sent to them by strangers, mainly from the USA. The daughter was 12 years old when I last saw the family. They gave me a photograph of themselves seated on a tractor looking fit and happy. I still possess it.

The Clywedog Dam

Soon after we settled in Llanidloes, the River Severn overflowed its banks along much of its length to Shrewsbury. This was a recurrent problem and, being the first town on the River Severn, Llanidloes was often affected by flood water, though on most occasions little damage was done. The main concern was with the geriatric unit. This was located by the river and, when the flood water reached the wards, the patients' safety was put at risk. Then they had to be evacuated to a safer place, usually to a small, derelict school that stood close to the cottage hospital. My first experience of evacuating the unit occurred on a cold autumnal day when the waters entered the wards. Again the local people dealt with the situation calmly and moved the patients away from the river bank. But the problem had become so recurrent that Parliament decided that it must be dealt with urgently, and in 1963 passed an Act ordering the construction of a dam across the River Clywedog, a major tributary which joined the River Severn above the town. The dam was intended to stop the river flooding in the winter and to maintain water levels in the summer. Construction work was soon started and the Clywedog Dam, together with a smaller dam needed to retain water close by, was completed in 1967. It was a massive project and was, at the time, the highest dam in Europe. It remains the tallest (72 metres high) mass concrete dam in Britain and its waters cover an area of 615 acres. Not surprisingly, its construction was opposed by local conservation groups including myself. I opposed it because the valley which was to be flooded was a beautiful and secluded area, and one of my favourite walks. There was almost a sense of prehistory to it, with the steep hills clothed with ferns and buzzards circling quietly overhead. At times I felt I was back 10,000 years, when my Welsh predecessors may have occupied the hill forts which are still discernible in outline today. Inevitably the dam flooded some farm buildings and fertile land has disappeared beneath the waters, but great care has been taken with the landscaping and the Clywedog Reservoir is now a beauty spot in its own right. The trout fishing is excellent, perhaps the best in Wales, and former American President, Jimmy Carter, has fished its waters. Its sailing club is another attraction, though my family's several attempts to launch and sail a Mirror dingy were usually pretty unsuccessful in the late 1960s.

I was asked to visit a farmhouse in the valley before the dam was built. It was being used as a holiday cottage and was occupied by a young girl and her mother who lacked the transport to attend the surgery. The track to the farm was so rough that I could not drive my car to the house so the farmer took me part of the way on his tractor. With him driving and me standing on the back of the tractor, holding my medical bag, we drove up the steep slope. It was not very safe. The tractor had no safety cab and the driver had syringomyelia, a disabling neurological disease. Syringomyelia forms cavities in the spinal cord – mainly in the neck region – which press on the spinal nerves, and produce sensory and motor losses in the arms and legs. The result is a wasting disease, affecting the muscles of the hands and legs together with a progressive loss of the ability to perceive pain and temperature. The farmer was a patient of ours and I knew him fairly well. He featured in an illustrated textbook on neurology written by a Dr Spillane, brother of the consultant psychiatrist I had known in Whitchurch Hospital, Cardiff. As a consequence of syringomyelia, the farmer also had a totally disrupted joint of the right elbow. Known as a Charcot joint, the bones appear fragmented on X-ray as if he had multiple fractures of the lower end of the humerus, but was completely painless. These disabilities did not deter him from driving his tractor on steep and slippery slopes. Travelling to the farm felt weird, partly because the Great Train Robbers were on the run and we were asked to look out for anyone unusual who might be hiding in isolated places. This sense of weirdness was heightened when I met the mother and daughter, and discovered their reason for the visit. They were nice intelligent folk but the purpose for my visit was singular. Aged about eleven, the girl had pierced her hymen with a sharp flint. She was alright, had caused no significant damage and no treatment was needed. I reassured the mother and departed, again somewhat nervously, on the back of the tractor.

Inevitably, the practice was involved with the construction of the dam, as we were the only practice close by. Some of the labour force was recruited locally, and were already patients of ours or adjoining practices; the remainder came mainly from Ireland and lived in wooden barracks nearby. Before work started, Severn Trent contacted Graham to ask him to give medical cover for the itinerant workforce and for any emergencies that arose. Naturally he said yes and we were paid the sum of £500 for the cover provided. Not much, but Graham was not a business man, and the partners accepted the agreement he had made. There were few serious incidents, and no fatalities on site, which was unusual for a construction project of that size. One gesture of local disapproval is worth noting. A bomb was detonated on the site in 1966, probably by Welsh nationalists, but that symbolic act delayed construction for only two months. Few other incidents stand out in my memory, though I was surprised that management made no effort to immunise or screen the workforce, and the wearing of hard hats became obligatory only towards the end of the project. I remember one young man who worked happily at height, but was epileptic and subject to fits which no one else seemed to be aware of. Eventually we sent him to a neurologist in London where, if I remember correctly, his father was a senior army officer with the Ministry of Defence. Another young man working on the site was schizophrenic. He had come from Ireland with an elder brother, who was a very capable man and took care of his younger sibling both on site and in the barracks. The younger man could do little useful work but no doubt the family back home were glad to see him obtain some work experience abroad.

Girlguiding Cymru

The war time association of Broneirion with Gordonstoun School has been mentioned already but in 1947 the house became an important centre for Girlguiding Cymru, the Girl Guide Association in Wales. This was due to the initiative of Lady (Eldrydd) Davies, the daughter-in-law of Lord Davies, who had brought Gordonstoun School to Llandinam. He died in 1944 and, in the same year, his son, a major in the Welsh Guards, died on active service in Europe. Broneirion was empty, as Plas Dinam, on the other side of the River Severn had become the family's main residence. The newly widowed Lady Davies had a keen interest in guiding and offered Broneirion, with 4.5 acres of land surrounding it, as the activity centre and 'Home for Guiding' for Wales. The offer was accepted and the house was officially opened by Lady Baden Powell in 1947. Within the grounds is Cae Gwenllian, a camping site, and Y Bwthyn the Brownies' house, which was once the summer house of the Davies children. In my time the centre was managed by an Australian lady, but although my wife was a Guide Commissioner, my association with Broneirion was simply medical. The recognised doctor for the centre was Graham Davies, though I would be asked to see any ailing Guides or Brownies in his absence. I recall seeing nothing serious; the girls and staff always appeared robust and happy. In 1992, Lord Davies decided to sell the house and Girlguiding Cymru purchased it the following year, together with the lodge and some additional land. It remains a thriving centre not just for Welsh Guides but for Guides from all over the world.

The River Wye in Flood

Caring for the soldiers who sometimes camped in the hills around Llanidloes was less predictable than caring for Girl Guides. The military tended to visit in the spring and summer months only, but even then the weather could be suddenly foul and problems with exposure and hypothermia would arise. Then, a safe haven for individual men would be needed, and their officers would seek the help of Llanidloes Hospital because they knew ours was the most likely unit to provide the stricken man with a warm bed and a good night's rest. One day, the River Wye overflowed and flooded a tented camp in Llangurig. About twenty soldiers were camping out that night and my help was sought, possibly because we were living nearby in the old Llangurig Vicarage, which I was renting. The men were soaked and needed shelter, but it was obvious we could not take them into the hospital as the staff could not have coped with so many men, so I discussed the situation with my wife. She agreed to take them in, and they were delighted to get indoors out of the cold and wet. There was a Rayburn stove in the kitchen and Valerie used this to provide hot drinks and to dry some of their clothes overnight. They left the next day, but the incident did not deter the army from returning to Llangurig the following year and camping again alongside the River Wye.

Our neighbour in Rhyader, Dr John Davies, telephoned me one night when I was in bed. The River Wye was in flood again and the weather was dreadful. A van had broken through the protective wall of a bridge on the Rhyader–Llangurig road and plunged into the river. John said that the driver and his passengers had been rescued, but those involved in the rescue, including himself, were exhausted. Could I help? The driver had been in the river for a long time and was on his way by ambulance to Llanidloes, but John needed to dry out and go to bed. So could I look after the man when he arrived at the hospital? I said yes of course. The driver was manager of a youth hostel in north Wales, which he was to have opened that day, and was travelling there with his wife, daughter and the daughter's boyfriend, when he lost control of their van on the bridge and it plunged into the river. The daughter and her boyfriend escaped through the rear door of the van and his wife through the passenger door, but the man was trapped in the driver's seat. The escapees raised the alarm and the rescue services were alerted. Police, fire brigade, ambulance men and GP all came to help but the driver could not be extricated, so a mobile crane was brought in to lift the vehicle out of the water. I cannot imagine how the crane was attached to the submerged van but it was done successfully and the van was lifted out of the water. This was the most critical moment for the trapped driver because the river flowed around his neck and he was able to keep his head above the water only by pressing downwards on his hands and arms. If the van had slipped when it was being raised, his head would have gone beneath the water and he would have drowned, but luckily all went well. On being extracted from the van, he was taken by ambulance to Llanidloes Hospital, where matron and I met him. He was remarkably phlegmatic and resilient; despite being in the water for hours, aware of the risk to his life and getting increasingly cold, he made little of it. We filled a bath with water, allowed him to adjust the temperature as he chose and then to soak in it for some time. He emerged when ready and was given a warm bed for the night. He left in the morning with his family and I heard no more about him. John Davies left his single-handed practice a few years later and joined the civil service as a medical officer in Bristol.

The Old People's Home

Dol-llys, a retirement home for older people, was situated a few miles outside Llanidloes. It was a Georgian house with extensive views and a charming matron to care for the residents. Some people found fault with its location, saying it should be situated in the town so that the residents could have easier access to shops and cafes, but I thought it was splendid. One night matron telephoned to tell me that one of her ladies was not well. I got out of bed, put on my red track suit and drove to Dol-llys where matron was waiting by the front door. She led me up the spiral staircase and into a small room where an elderly lady lay on a bed, gasping for breath. She was desperately ill, breathless, cyanosed and comatose. I was not equipped to deal with such an emergency. I had no oxygen and little in my medical bag that would help apart from one ampoule of aminophylline, so I gave her all the aminophylline intravenously. That made the situation worse. She began to vomit and her breathing became more laboured. We placed her head and shoulders over the edge of the bed so she would not inhale the vomit and, when the vomiting ceased, made her as safe and comfortable as possible. I did not expect her to survive the night, so I sat on the edge of the bed and said a silent prayer, then we left. Before departing, I turned to matron and said, "ring me in the morning and tell me how she is" and thinking that I'd let her have the death certificate then. Matron telephoned during the morning surgery and I immediately said "I will bring the death certificate to you". "There is no need to do that," she replied, "she is fine, fully recovered". I was surprised. A few weeks later, I visited Dol-llys to see another patient, but did not realise it would be my last visit to the home despite having arranged to leave the practice and move to a new job in London. It was the last time that I was to see the sick lady of my previous visit. We did not speak, but I can still picture her standing at the top of the stairs, smiling down as I stood in the hall chatting with matron.

Another incident associated with Dol-llys concerned a retired postman. He was an elderly man who had delivered mail to the farms and hamlets around Llanidloes for many years. He had no transport, not even a bicycle, and his work was done on foot. There would have been many beautiful days for walking the hills when the work would be enjoyable, but there would be many wet and miserable days too, when he would be glad to get back home. He lived alone and I sometimes marvelled at his ability to walk the distances he did. Eventually, he retired and soon afterwards developed temporal arteritis, a painful condition of the arteries which can cause sudden blindness. Treatment with prednisolone proved effective but he was becoming frail and asked to be admitted to Dol-llys. Matron telephoned me about his application to be admitted. She said a room was available but before admitting him she needed the consent of a member of the management committee and asked me to speak to Sir George Hamer, a local magnate and a member of the committee, to authorise the admission. I had not met Sir George but we knew one another by reputation, so I phoned him and explained the situation, and asked for his permission for matron to admit the postman. Sir George was courteous and helpful and said "Of course Dr Rees, tell matron that she can take him in" which I did. This was probably during the very hard winter of 1963 as there must have been a very pressing reason for admitting the man so urgently. When I spoke to Sir George I did not realise that he was a sick man, as he was a patient of the other practice before the two local practices were united. He died a few days later and I have always admired the concern he showed for this other elderly man when he himself was on his own death bed. I learnt from matron later that the postman had arrived with few possessions, but he did bring two large suitcases that he would not let her open. Eventually she managed to look inside and found them packed with bank notes. I believe the total value was about £10,000, which she persuaded him to take to a bank, and deposit in a safer place than an old people's home.

Night Visits

Night visits were a normal part of a GP's work in the 20th century. Many were to sick children and sometimes I would hear the child crying in the background as the mother spoke on the telephone. Some requests were bizarre, like the call to visit a man because "his eye was popping out". I might have said "give him an aspirin and bring him to the surgery in the morning", but that was not our way and our patients rarely requested visits for frivolous reasons. So I put on the red tracksuit that I wore for night visits, left Valerie alone in bed, and went to see my patient. There was considerable consternation in a usually peaceful household, as the man's left eye was protruding though not popping out. He had a proptosis of his left eye that was of recent origin. Something serious was happening but there was nothing to do that night, except to reassure the family and see him again when I had discussed the situation with Graham Davies. He suggested referring the man to a neurologist in London, which I did. He was referred as a private patient and a brain scan showed that there was a tumour in the left frontal lobe and it was pushing the eye forward. The tumour was removed surgically and proved to be benign. The man returned home with a normal looking eye and normal eyesight. It was a good result and he had no further trouble with his eye or tumour.

Two night visits were to people who went to bed, then died unexpectedly. One man was in his early sixties. He died suddenly from a heart attack with his wife lying alongside him. I have little recollection of my visit, apart from seeing him in the bed, and talking to his widow. She was totally numbed by his death. Not tearful, not agitated, scarcely able to believe what had happened. I believe she was alone in the house when I arrived, but that family and friends came to support her whilst I was there. The other death was just as sudden, though even more unusual. Again, I was summoned from bed, put on my track suit and went to a terraced house that was occupied by a member of the St John Ambulance Brigade and his wife, a regular worshipper at the parish church. The front door opened into a small hallway with the staircase facing the door, and a sitting room to the right of the entrance. The husband took me into the sitting room where his wife lay on a small sofa. They had gone to bed as usual, but soon after retiring to bed she went downstairs for no apparent reason. There she called up to her husband: "Come down quickly, I am dying, I can see Jesus." He hurried down to her but there was nothing he could do. She was dead, and cardiopulmonary resuscitation (CPR) was not taught or practised then. Unusually, no one was available in the town who could lay her out. The local undertaker did not provide that service, and the district nurses were not allowed to do so as they were midwives. So I laid out her body as best I could, and found undertaking this final act very moving.

Clergy and Chapels

Tom Williams the vicar of Llanidloes was a keen fisherman and beekeeper. He had a large garden – too big he would say – where he kept beehives. One morning his wife phoned to say he had been stung by a swarm of bees and needed to be seen urgently. So I went. The front door of the vicarage was open so I walked in and found the vicar collapsed at the bottom of the staircase; he had been collecting the swarm and was badly stung. I knelt beside him to assess how best to treat him, when a man came from the back kitchen and stood beside us. It was John Price, the local handyman and undertaker. "Is there anything I can do to help, doctor?" John asked. I was surprised that an undertaker should happen to be present and to ask that question at such a time, but the vicar's condition was not life-threatening and he was not in need of John's expertise as an undertaker, so I was pleased to reply "No thank you John". Tom Williams had collapsed but his airway was clear and he needed time to recover. I gave him an injection of chlorphenamine and hydrocortisone, and admitted him to hospital for observation. He made a good recovery and returned home the next day.

The Rev. Tom Williams became vicar of Llanidloes just two weeks before I settled in the town and became a regular attendee at the parish church. At first I could not understand why he found so many faults with his congregation in his sermons and why they tolerated it, but I soon learnt the reason. He had not wanted to come to Llanidloes. He had been very content in his previous parish, at Pwllheli, where he enjoyed working with the holiday-makers and living in a Welsh-speaking part of Wales. Llanidloes was more anglicised and the church had no services in Welsh. Tom had reluctantly accepted the transfer because the bishop was keen for him to do so, and the appointment to Llanidloes was the gift of the bishop. For my part, apart from attending service on Sunday, I did not expect to become closely involved with the Church – that I did so was due mainly to Tom Williams. I had not taken the sacraments for many years, but in due course became a regular communicant, churchwarden, member of the deanery and diocesan synods, and a member of the governing body of the Church in Wales. I was also appointed a minister of the sacrament for the great festivals of Easter and Christmas, an unusual privilege for a lay person in the 1960s, though quite common today. Tom and I had arrived at Llanidloes within a fortnight of each other and departed within the same space of time. He became vicar of Criccieth in north Wales and I joined the Civil Service Department in London. Later, when we moved to Warwickshire, I went to a Sunday service at All Saints Parish Church in Leamington Spa and was warmly welcomed by the vicar, Idwal Jones. When he learnt that I had lived in Llanidloes and had attended the church where his brother was vicar before Tom Williams, he insisted that I should become a member of his congregation, which I did. Such an interesting association between the two churches reminded me again of Jung's teaching on synchronicity.

Carl Jung was interested in the deeper structures of the human psyche including their religious significance. His contemporary, Sigmund Freud, was different – he delved less deeply into the human psyche, and though Jewish by birth, was an atheist by conviction. He wrote a book on jokes, intending it to be a serious assessment of humour, and through it his name is associated with the verbal slips that people sometimes make inadvertently. One churchgoer in Llanidloes tended to make a typical Freudian slip when we met. He visited the surgery only occasionally, but if he did so, he was as likely to address me as vicar (then apologise for the mistake) as call me doctor. This is not an unusual mistake, at times I have been called father, brother, bishop, doctor, and vicar but, though a Christian, I am not an evangelist. I have no desire to convert others to my beliefs, though happy to discuss them with anyone who wishes to do so. On the domestic front, my wife started to accompany me to church only in Llanidloes, and she then brought the children with her until they were aged 16 when they made up their own minds. We have three children: Eileen, Anna and David. Our son was conceived in Llangurig and born in Abernant. It was not an easy birth, though not difficult in an obstetric sense. Anna had flu at the time and Valerie was possibly affected by it when she went into labour. I've always admired the way that Val not only coped with giving birth when she was not well herself, but that she also struggled to get off her bed to care for Anna. She was delivered by Nurse Davies, and Tom Brittain was also present at David's birth. This was one of the many times when I have considered the courage and tenacity of women as mothers to be extraordinary.

Occasionally, I was asked to take services in Nonconformist chapels. I never sought the role, but it began when St Luke's Day happened to fall on a Sunday. Tom Williams asked me to preach the sermon that evening, which I agreed to do only because I find it easier to say yes than no if asked to do something difficult. The sermon was scheduled for a Sunday when the Blood Transfusion Service was visiting the town, and, after church, many of us went to the community hall to donate a pint of blood. Graham was already there, as he liked to help, and had given and taken blood for many years. That year about 150 pints were donated, a remarkable amount for a small market town (population approximately 2,000) and its surrounding countryside. I gave a pint of blood and wondered if it was a good thing to do before preaching a first sermon. This was carefully prepared and written but, as I ascended the pulpit that evening, I was very nervous. The congregation was much larger than usual and had come, in part from curiosity, to see how the new doctor was going to cope with a role no other doctor had undertaken in living memory in the parish, if ever. It went alright. I might have been a little elated afterwards with the loss of blood and the job completed, but it was over and I was glad it was done. I did not expect the follow-up. A few weeks later, two deacons from the English Baptist Chapel came to my surgery with a request. The conversation went something like this: "Doctor, you know we have no minister at the moment and are in the process of appointing one, but we have no one to take the services in the next few weeks. Will you help us and take an evening service for us?" I was flattered, surprised and said yes; at least I had a sermon that could be used again, but would have to prepare the rest of the service, the readings and prayers, and possibly the hymns. It was a big requirement, for I was very busy and had no experience in leading a service or even praying in public. Again the evening went reasonably well and the congregation was larger than normal but I was not prepared for the comments that followed. In the Baptist chapel, it was customary for the evening to end with a senior deacon saying a few words about the service. The appointed deacon summarised my effort by saying, in effect, "it is a pity more of you were not here this morning because the preacher was Mr Harris, the headmaster, and we had a wonderful service". His comments were helpfully deflating, but my role as an itinerant preacher continued for a while as I had other invitations from chapels in the hills and even for an annual Lenten visit to the English Baptist Chapel after their new minister was appointed.

Some people tell me that I should have been a priest. One dear old lady in Llangurig used to say whenever we met, "You should be a *ficer*". For her it was a much more elevated role than being a doctor, but that was fifty years ago and she was 92 years old though still as bright as a button. It was a pleasure to visit her in the farmhouse where she was born and lived with her bachelor brother, both cared for by Alfred, a young man from the village. The possibility of being ordained had occurred, but on full consideration I knew it was not for me. I doubt too if Val would have wanted to be a vicar's wife, though I am sure she would have been a good one. Moreover, my personal belief is not sectarian, it tends towards the ecumenical and inter-faith, and I was fortunate in the range of friendships that I enjoyed with the clergy in Llanidloes. I was particularly close to the Catholic priest (Fr Kenneth Gillespie) and an Orthodox priest (Archimandrite Barnabus). Perhaps because they were celibates they enjoyed the family support that Valerie and I gave them more than most people. Fr Barnabus and his two young monks shared some very happy meals with us, whilst Fr Gillespie would drop in on a Wednesday evening for a *craic* over a glass of whisky and some pipe tobacco. When the evening was over, I would watch him stagger to his car and drive home, fortunately along the mainly empty roads of Llanidloes. He was a popular man in the town and became mayor of Llanidloes.

Archimandrite Barnabus

Archimandrite Barnabus was a Welsh-speaking Welshman who was born in Pennal and attended the old Towyn County School (now Ysgol Uwchradd Tywyn) which, because of its remote catchment area, then catered for boarders. It must have been a remarkable school as it produced many doctors and three influential men who I knew personally. One was the senior cardiologist at St Thomas's Hospital, another was my own Professor of Anatomy, and the third was Barnabus. Fr Barnabus was a particularly interesting man and, although he died in 1996, is already being called "the founding father of Orthodoxy in Wales". He was christened Richard Burton and was originally an Anglican priest (and a minor canon at Bangor Cathedral) with a High Church bent. He converted to the Roman Catholic Church in the 1930s and was sent to teach at Douai School as a layman, but he was not happy there as he knew that his true vocation was to be a priest. After World War II he met a charismatic Orthodox priest (Père Denis Chambault) in Paris, joined the Western Rite Church and was ordained as a priest in the Russian Orthodox Church, within which he became an archimandrite, a priest monk. His ultimate aim was to establish a permanent monastic community in Wales and to bring Orthodoxy back to his native land. In these endeavours he was only partially successful.

In due course, during the late 1960s, Barnabus established a small monastic community in a farmhouse at Tyllwch, near Llanidloes. The farm was at the end of a steep rough track that was difficult to negotiate, and it was at Llanidloes Hospital that I first met Sergei Armstone, one of his two novice monks. I asked if I could visit the monastery and he said "Yes, you would be very welcome" – my family and that small community soon became close friends. For financial reasons, the Tyllwch project did not last long and the house was closed, Sergei eventually becoming an Orthodox priest and the other novice, Phillip Roderick, an Anglican priest and founder of the Quiet Garden Movement. Fr Barnabus had to move into a house at New Chapel where he lived alone but continued saying all the monastic offices each day. If free I would join him for some of the offices, a companionship that he encouraged if only for those brief occasions. He spent one Christmas day with us and I remember two things about the occasion. As soon as he sat down, he wanted to look at the *Radio Times*, to check on the television programmes which he loved watching. He insisted also on saying the daily offices, and I would say them with him in the dining room, leaving the room with a slight smell of incense. Whilst he was at New Chapel, deacons from the local Baptist Chapel came to me one day to ask if I would conduct a service for them at New Chapel. I had done so once before but now enquired if they had asked Fr Barnabus to help. As they said no, I suggested that they invite him and, if they had any problems, I would step in. A few weeks later Val and I attended the evening service Fr Barnabus conducted at New Chapel. This was the first time he had been asked to preach in a Nonconformist chapel in Wales and it was, I think, the prelude to much else, as he received other invitations to preach and appeared regularly on Welsh-language radio and television programmes. One other recollection comes to mind. As a member of the governing body of the Church in Wales, I invited him and his monks to be my guest at the annual synod, which was held then in a cinema in Llandrindod Wells with visitors sitting in the balcony upstairs. We had a meal in one of the hotels and during the meal various bishops, including the archbishop, came to speak to him. I thought that was so courteous, and indicative of the friendly support that I believe the Church in Wales continues to show to Orthodoxy.

Eventually Fr Barnabus moved to New Mills where he built his own chapel and we were able to meet only occasionally. A few days before our last meeting, I had a strong urge to go to a small Orthodox chapel that had been established in Rugby by a former Anglican priest. I attended the liturgy that Sunday and found to my surprise that Fr Barnabus was the presiding priest. At the end of the service I joined other members of the congregation in going to the priest and kissing the crucifix held in his hand. As I did so, he looked at me and said "Oh it is you. I must come and see Valerie tomorrow and have one of her lunches", which he did, together with the Anglican priest who had driven him from Wales. It was good to see him in such a convivial mood. He died some months later.

Hippies and Quakers

I had many patients who belonged to hippie communes. Some followed the teachings of Ouspensky and Gurdjieff but most were flower people – dropouts if you like – who were seeking a spiritual path that suited their own lifestyle. Among them was John Shepherd who, with his American wife and infant son Padma, had fled in an old van from an Eastern guru in London, and travelled westwards until they found a cottage in Trefeglwys and settled there. They were not attached to a church or religious group but were spiritual people whose lifestyle included a vegetarian diet, no alcohol and no smoking. One evening they invited Val and me to their cottage for dinner and were particularly proud of the water they gave us; it had been collected on Midsummer's day from a well near Glastonbury Tor and was considered to possess special healing and spiritual properties. Eventually, they left to explore the music of the Andes and the spiritual traditions of native Indians in the Americas. They maintained contact with me for some years, but I never had their address and could not reply.

Another resident of the town was an old lady whose parents had died when the *Titanic* sank. I cannot remember if she was also on the ship when it went down, but I know she was brought up by close relatives, probably an aunt. Her parents were of the Quaker faith, but her aunt was Anglican, and the little girl was christened and confirmed within the Church of England. She remained with the church throughout her life and was a regular attendee at St Idloes Parish Church when I knew her. Because of her Quaker roots, she had always wanted to go to a Quaker meeting but had never managed to do so, so I promised to take her one day. There was a lovely Friends Meeting House in Newtown about ten miles away, and occasionally I would attend the meetings for worship. Not many people used to go, usually about six or eight, and once there were just two of us. But they were always good occasions with people just sitting quietly together, then having coffee and perhaps a sandwich when the meeting (which lasted an hour) ended. One Sunday morning, in an impulsive moment, I knocked on the old lady's door and said, "I am going to take you to the Quaker meeting". She was surprised and said, "I cannot come, I've got my dinner in the oven". "Oh do turn it off", I said, "and come along", which she did. She said that she had a lovely time. The friends in the meeting house made a great fuss of her and she fulfilled an ambition held for much of her life.

The Big Freeze

Another friend was the Rev. D J Owen, minister of the Welsh Methodist Church in Llangurig. He was a farmer's son, honest and helpful, and used to drive around the villages on a motorcycle with sidecar, in which his wife Meg and two sons sometimes travelled with him. Known as D J, he was a pipe smoker and would stride into my surgery for medicines for his chest, accompanied by a strong smell of tobacco. He had a big voice and preached with equal facility in English and Welsh without the need for an amplifying system. We were neighbours for a few months and got to know each other particularly well during the winter of 1962–3, when I was renting the old rectory in Llangurig whilst waiting to move into Abernant. It was a very cold winter, with heavy snowfalls in most parts of the country, causing chaos in the hills and blocking many roads. Graham was incapacitated, and I was doing most of the extra work that that entailed. The countryside was beautiful. The rime frost on the trees and hedges was spectacular and I remember two visitors from overseas, who had thumbed a lift in the car, saying "it is like fairy land". As I travelled around the practice, I usually had the roads to myself, which lessened the risk of colliding with other motorists. Despite the gritting, our rural A roads were reduced to a single lane in many areas, and my Ford Anglia would skid into the snow banks almost contentedly and without affecting my progress much. Problems did arise, possibly because my driving was not immaculate. Sometimes I skidded into ditches even when there was little snow or ice to blame. Then men would appear almost miraculously and lift the car out of the ditch and set me on my way again. Once I crashed into an approaching car on a mountain corner. I cannot say it was entirely my fault but it was not a good move as the car belonged to matron, and the driver was her brother. I got the impression she was not best pleased.

The weather in January 1963 was so cold that the temperature did not rise above freezing point in the daytime and remained as low as –15°C at night. Our house in Llangurig had no central heating and our supply of water was soon frozen – for six weeks we were without running water. Fortunately D J and Meg lived nearby, their tap water was not affected and, whilst the freeze persisted, they kept us supplied with water, bringing it to the rectory in buckets. They were always cheerful and helped to keep Val's spirits up whilst she was alone in the house and I was busy with the patients. During that very cold spell, there was no increase in the incidence of illness. In fact we were asked to see fewer people than usual. This was partly due to people's reluctance to trouble the doctor when conditions were so difficult and also, perhaps, because the germs remained quiescent whilst the temperatures were so low. People were also inclined to stay indoors during the cold spell which reduced the likelihood of their falling on the ice-cold paths and pavements. Once the weather broke, the requests for help escalated and people suddenly became ill with bronchitis and other complaints that the cold weather had suppressed.

Resuscitating the Dead

The weather was improving when I received a request to visit an old man at Hafodfraith, a farmhouse near Llangurig. The request came as I was about to start my morning surgery at Abernant. There were only a few people in the waiting room and I thought I could deal with them quickly, then nip up to the farm before going to the surgery at Caersws. But I did not manage to see all the patients waiting until it was time to go to Caersws, which was in the opposite direction from Hafodfraith. So, with an uncertain heart, I decided to go to Caersws first, and had dealt with all the patients in Glenys's house when the telephone rang. It was Miss Parry. She was phoning to say that the situation at Hafodfraith had become very urgent and I was needed immediately. I left at once and, as I drove to the distant farmhouse, I sent up an arrow prayer (a silent urgent prayer) that the man would be alive when I reached him.

I drove as fast as possible but when I left the tarmac road and saw Alan Jones of Ystradolwen holding a gate open for me, I knew the situation was really critical. My concern increased when I reached Hafodfraith. The man standing at the front door looked so sad that I knew my patient was dead. I said nothing to him but went into the house, saw an old lady sitting on a settle by the kitchen fire, and I knew also from her appearance that the old farmer had died. We said nothing but I rushed upstairs and into the nearest bedroom where a middle-aged woman stood gazing at a man lying on a bed. He was very still and obviously dead. I asked how long he had been like this and learnt that it was just for a few minutes, so I hurried to him and began external cardiac massage which was not a normal procedure at the time. To my surprise, he began to breathe spontaneously, and his heart began to beat, perceptibly and regularly. He remained unconscious but he was alive and my prayer had been answered; I had brought some relief to the family and they would not have to experience the ordeal of a coroner's inquest and, even more importantly, a sudden bereavement. In the meantime Mr Davies required expert nursing care but I knew I could not get him into hospital. The beds at Llanidloes Hospital were full and the road to Aberystwyth was blocked, so there was no possibility of getting him to Bronglais Hospital, so he had to remain at home. I placed him in the recovery position, raised the foot of his bed on a chair and gave him an injection of the antibiotic, chloramphenicol. Then I left, telling the family that I would return as soon as possible but that I would have to see my other patients first, and that I would send Nurse Davies (the district nurse) to help them as soon as she was free.

The rest of the day is a bit of a blur but, when I returned to Hafodfraith that evening, Mr Davies was showing signs of recovery. Nurse Davies had arrived and the mood in the house had changed completely. The next morning, he looked very good. He was alert, cheerful and smoking his pipe. I was delighted because he was alive and the family was happy, but there was another more selfish reason.

Cardiac resuscitation was not common in the early 1960s. Successes for external cardiac massage were being reported from hospitals but not often, and not from outside their walls, most certainly not from isolated farmhouses or on people in their eighties, as was the case with Mr Davies. His recovery was very unusual and merited a report in a medical journal. I was sufficiently certain that my patient had died from a heart attack that I had taken an electrocardiogram to the house to confirm that possibility, but the ECG's electrical plug did not fit the sockets in the farmhouse, so that conclusive evidence could not be obtained. However, I had sent blood to the laboratory at Bronglais Hospital to check his cardiac enzymes.

Mr Davies continued to make steady progress over the next few days. He was a real character, full of pleasantries and jokes and constantly badgering us to let him get up. The results of the blood tests arrived after a few days and were interesting. He had an SGOT level of 186, which supported my provisional diagnosis of coronary thrombosis, and a blood urea of 80mgms/100 mls, that indicated the kidneys were not functioning perfectly though this could improve. The blood reports arrived on a Saturday, the same day of the week as his unexpected death. After seeing my patients in Caersws, I drove to Hafodfraith feeling slightly elated, partly because it was a lovely day and I hoped to see a recovering patient, but also because I could now publish an interesting paper in a medical journal. When I reached the house I entered a déjà vu situation and knew that things had gone suddenly wrong. Mr Davies's nephew was standing outside the farmhouse looking terribly sad. The old lady was sitting in the kitchen showing no animation in her face or posture. The person standing in the bedroom gazing down at the body was not his niece on this occasion, but Nurse Davies, who told me that the old man was brighter than ever when she arrived that morning. She had made him comfortable and gone downstairs. A few minutes later the nephew called to her, "Come up quick", and when she reached the bedroom the old man was gasping for breath and died almost immediately. Soon afterwards I arrived. Mr Davies had been dead for only a few minutes but I did not try to revive him again. If he had lived longer, I would have enquired about any death bed experiences he may have had. For instance, if he had a sense of travelling at speed towards a light, or had met people previously known to him, as reported by others who, though close to death, had subsequently recovered. But I had waited too long. He was buried three days later.

District Nurses

The district nurses who cared for our patients at home were Nurse Davies and Olwen Hamer. Both were trained nurses and midwives. Nurse Davies, who was the oldest, was always addressed as nurse, whilst Olwen Hamer was always Olwen. Her husband was a local man and she may have been local too, which would help to explain the greater familiarity. Both were excellent nurses and well integrated within the community. Olwen was the midwife who attended the births in the pantechnicon at Staylittle and at the Lion Hotel in Llandinam which have been mentioned already. Nurse Davies was the midwife when my son David was born in Abernant, in 1963. She also cared for my parents when they were terminally ill the following year. My mother's illness was a surprise. She was only 64 when Dr Monroe, our family doctor in Barry, phoned to let me know that my mother had abdominal cancer. I took her to a consultant in Cardiff who insisted, in the nicest possible way, on referring her to a surgeon for a biopsy and then for radiotherapy in Oxford, though it was obvious that the outlook was grim. My parents could not manage at home alone and needed to come to live with us, but we were still in Llangurig and had not expected to move into Abernant so soon. Thus although it was very inconvenient for Graham and his wife, they kindly agreed to move into temporary accommodation whilst Dyfnant Villa, on the outskirts of the town, was being renovated for them. I still appreciate their helpfulness in moving so promptly. Valerie was brilliant and my parents could not have had a better daughter-in-law during that difficult time. My father was twelve years older than mother and, as her condition deteriorated, he became very upset and died six weeks before her. Yet she still got out of her sick bed to tend him even though she was in pain and wasting away. The day he died I delivered a baby in the hospital. It was the mother's first baby and though she had normal contractions she experienced no pain. The labour progressed well but when the cervix was fully dilated she could do nothing to assist the progress of the baby, and needed help. Graham gave the anaesthetic (chloroform on a gauze mask) and I applied mid-cavity forceps. Everything went smoothly and I delivered a boy child who, very much in the tradition of the area, was christened Graham. I learnt from the grandmother later that the family believed Graham had delivered the baby and that I gave the anaesthetic. It was good to have helped a baby into this world as my father was leaving it. When mother died a few weeks later, I was the only person with her and it was exceptionally moving. Valerie was a huge support to me in my grief, but I continued to work after the deaths and the only days I had off were when my parents were buried. Valerie had a high opinion of Nurse Davies, who was such an important person in our lives and, having tasted the nurse's apple chutney, liked it so much that she asked for the recipe. Subsequently, every year before Christmas, the smell of Cox's Orange Pippin apples cooking on the stove would fill our kitchen, because we all loved Nurse Davies' chutney.

When Nurse Davies retired she was replaced by an excellent nurse whose name I cannot remember, though I can picture her clearly. She was also the health visitor and tended to appear at evening surgeries with patients she wanted me to see. One was a woman who had been badly beaten by her husband. They were a farming family with children at school in the day and no neighbours close enough to notice any domestic disharmony. He was having an affair with a married woman, his wife discovered the liaison and, when she complained, he beat her. Though badly bruised she had the good sense to contact the nurse and let her know what had happened. Nurse brought the woman to see me, and I placed a record of the events in her notes in case she decided to divorce or take legal action. I heard nothing further about the incident or of their relationship as a married couple.

It seems likely that the new district nurse, being a health visitor, had a close association with the local school, probably attending clinics there with the Assistant Medical Officer of Health, though I cannot recall how this was organised. What I do know is that Llanidloes had two excellent schools, a primary school and a comprehensive school, sharing the same campus. My three children all attended these schools and received the excellent academic grounding that parents desire for their offspring. The teachers were well integrated into the local community and on one famous occasion two (or possibly three) teachers played for the local football side when Llanidloes Town FC won the Welsh Cup. Clinics were held in the school by the Assistant Medical Officer of Health, as mentioned, who occasionally contacted me if she was referring a child to a specialist clinic for assessment. One child was my daughter Eileen, who wanted her tonsils to be removed, something I resisted because I considered it a painful procedure that did little to stop children having sore throats. Anyway, Eileen was referred to the ENT surgeon by the school doctor and had her tonsils removed in Wrexham Hospital.

Incest and Rape

Without delving into details, one case of incest and three of rape were related to me by my patients. One attractive teenager was made pregnant by her father and carried his child to term. Throughout the pregnancy the daughter said nothing about the father and revealed her infant's parentage only because she could not obtain any payments from the Social Service until she did so. When his identity was disclosed the father sadly committed suicide. Another teenager was assaulted and raped when walking along a country lane. She reported the incident to me and named the young man, whom I could readily associate with such an act. She was very upset and I advised her to report the matter to the police, which she did, but then decided not to proceed with any charges. The next victim was an older woman, who had already informed one of my partners and probably the police of the rape, before coming to me. She told her stories with difficulty, but said she had been attacked twice by the same man in an outhouse and, as they were both horse people, the possibility of their being in a barn together seems likely. I do not know why she decided to come to me as, apart from listening and reinforcing previous advice, there was little I could do to help. The final incident happened before I came to Llanidloes, and I was possibly the first person to be told about it. The woman was a middle-aged widow who consulted me for another reason, but during the consultation told me, almost in passing, that she had been raped by her brother-in-law soon after her husband's death. Her husband was a farmer, and about six weeks after the funeral his brother visited her when she was alone on the farm in what seemed, at first, to be an innocuous visit; then he raped her. Although I cannot be sure she had not informed anyone else, one thing was certain, her contempt and hatred for her brother-in-law was very real.

Suicides

Suicides are more common among doctors and in farming communities than in most other groups. I have mentioned the death of Spot Jenkins already and will explain the suicide of another doctor later, but here I will discuss only those people who were patients of the Llanidloes practice. One which occurred before I joined the practice was a particularly sad event, as it was the suicide of a young mother who had left her two children orphaned with only their elderly father to care for them on an isolated hill farm. I saw the father only occasionally. Once, when I was asked to visit a child at the farm, I remember his intense anger because he thought I was late in getting there. Subsequently, at a Monday morning surgery, I was awaiting my next patient when the door opened and a 12-year-old boy entered the room leading his father by the hand. It was the widower and his son. The man could not see, he was completely blind and needed to be helped into the chair by my desk. He said his vision was fine until the previous afternoon, when he was dealing with the Sunday school accounts, and suddenly lost the sight in both eyes. He was quite phlegmatic about it. "Why did you not call me?" I asked. "Because there was nothing you could do" he said. He was quite right, but I did know a doctor who could do something and he was in Llanidloes Hospital that morning. He was our consultant ophthalmic surgeon and when I phoned him he agreed to see the farmer immediately. He examined the man and found that he had a retinal haemorrhage in one eye and a mature cataract in the other. Nothing could be done about the haemorrhage in his previously good eye, but the cataract could be treated. He admitted the man to his unit that day and replaced the cataract with a plastic lens. As a consequence, the man regained the vision he had before the retinal haemorrhage, though with a different eye, and he was well-pleased with the result.

Another elderly farmer hanged himself in a tree, and Police Sergeant Davies alerted Dr Graham and myself. Graham went to the body and I went to support the family. When I entered the farmhouse kitchen, there were about six or seven adults sitting in a circle saying nothing. There were no tears, just total silence. I sat with them and maintained the silence they had chosen. We sat together quietly for a long time then I spoke. I said nothing inspirational but the silence was broken and someone asked me to give the widow a sleeping draught. I said I would, if she wanted it, but she said no, a decision we accepted. I left them sitting quietly together and did not anticipate what followed. Throughout the night, the widow kept running outside and screaming "Why did you leave me?" No one slept that night and everyone was exhausted in the morning. Eventually the widow went to bed and slept. She never looked back; I expected her to be full of grief but she wasn't. It was as if, by running out to scream in the darkness, she had healed herself of the pain of that sudden death. It was probably therapeutic, as I know of other people who, when dreadfully bereft, have found solace in going to a lonely place where they can scream aloud undeterred.

A World War II veteran, who had fought the Japanese in Burma, also killed himself. I remember standing alongside him during the annual Remembrance Day parade on 11 November. This was an important occasion in Llanidloes with members of the British Legion assembling outside the town hall, where they were marshalled by Sergeant Davies and joined by members of the borough council, including my wife Valerie, before marching to the parish church to the music of the town band. I stood chatting to this veteran, watching the parade pass by on an occasion when the elected town mayor had been a conscientious objector (a Conchie as they were called in those days) during the war, and not served in the army. The mayor was a good man and an excellent councillor, but the old soldier's bitterness at the mayor's elevated status in the town, compared with his own, was great. I thought little about it at the time, and was surprised to be called to his shop sometime later to find him hanging from a beam. I went to see his wife in an adjoining room. She was chatting to a neighbour and I said something inconsequential to her. "Poor bugger" she replied and continued chatting. I left and prepared a report for the coroner.

Schizophrenia and a Family Tragedy

Sioned was a young woman with epilepsy; she also had schizophrenia. Sometimes, she would be found dazed by the roadside following a fit, but she was always cheerful. Then I referred her to a psychiatrist who admitted her to hospital and tried to control her symptoms. He was a Welsh-speaking doctor and I chose him because Sioned's family spoke Welsh in the home and I thought it would be helpful, but her condition deteriorated and further admissions to the psychiatric unit were needed. I was asked to see her once after the family had moved from a large house to a secluded cottage. When I arrived at the cottage Sioned was upstairs sitting on a window ledge and I went up to see her. As I entered the bedroom she told me that she was a goddess and that I was to kneel down and adore her, otherwise she would throw herself off the window ledge to the ground below. I do not remember the rest of the conversation, but managed to talk her off the window and she was returned to the psychiatric unit.

Another time I was asked to see her late at night when the moon was full. This was a different house, not the riverside cottage but an old farmhouse with a huge fireplace in the living room – the fireplace was so big that they could burn tree trunks in it and did. The entrance door was close to the road on a hill, and I walked straight into the living room after leaving my car. Sioned and her mother were waiting for

143

me in the living room, with Sioned wearing her nightdress but nothing on her feet, and holding a slipper in her hand. As I entered the room she hit me across the face with the slipper, then ran out of the house and along the road up the hill with me in pursuit. Luckily there was no passing traffic; it was a moonlit night and any transient observer would have been amazed and probably worried to see a young woman attired only in a nightdress running up the hill in bare feet from a man intent on catching her. I did manage to grab her, and holding her firmly ran her down the hill into the house, up the stairs to her room, and gave her a large dose of chlorpromazine by IM (intramuscular) injection. Then I returned home to bed. We had no community psychiatric nurses to visit her in those days, but I believe she returned to the psychiatric unit the next day. After I left the area, she had an epileptic fit close to the fireplace and was badly burnt, dying of her injuries in Birmingham Accident Hospital some weeks later.

I knew Sioned's family well and remember observing an idyllic scene outside their cottage whilst walking across some nearby fields. It was a truly romantic sight. A young couple were sitting close together, enjoying each other's company as he played his guitar for her delight. Their closeness has always stayed in my mind, and became especially moving when a week or so later I received an urgent call from the young woman, Sioned's sister Enid, to say that her companion was unconscious in the cottage and she could not wake him. I left immediately and told her to send for the ambulance, but I reached the cottage before the ambulance and was met at the door by Enid. She said, "Dewi, I think he is dead" and took me up a spiral staircase to a room where a young Asian man lay on the bed unconscious. His heart was beating and he was breathing, so thankfully he was alive, but clearly in a poor way as he had taken an overdose of sleeping tablets. The ambulance arrived soon afterwards and I arranged for him to be admitted to the Shrewsbury hospital where he worked as a medical registrar. I supervised his transfer from bed to ambulance very carefully, not letting them carry him downstairs in a chair, but insisting that he was placed on a flexible stretcher and ensuring that his airway was kept open. In that way he reached the ambulance safely and was taken to hospital accompanied by Enid. He made a good recovery overnight and discharged himself from hospital the next day. Sadly his unconscious state had been a deliberate suicide attempt. He was a well-qualified young doctor from the Indian subcontinent who was determined to marry Enid but, although she liked him very much, she did not intend to marry him or any other man. I knew that, and her reasons for holding that view, but he would not accept any refusal from her. He swore that if she did not marry him, he would make another, this time successful attempt at suicide. The family asked me to speak to him, but I had seen him only on those two brief occasions; moreover, he had already moved to the north-east of England, and I did not feel that I could have a useful discussion with him on the telephone. He killed himself some months later.

Enid also committed suicide some years after I left Llanidloes. It was so sad; she was such a lively and talented woman. In addition to being a trained nurse, she was a notable artist and, when I left the area, she gave me a woodcut of the Clywedog Dam, which she had designed and made herself. The subject had personal associations, as I first met Enid when visiting her grandfather, a patriarchal nonagenarian who spoke only Welsh, at the farm where they lived, close to the intended dam. It was a memorable visit, as the house was said to be the meeting place of the first Sunday school to have been held in Wales, perhaps in the world. However, when Enid gave me the woodcut, which I still have in my study, I was horrified. Artistically it is excellent, but my overwhelming impression on receiving it was of its darkness, and of the sadness it revealed within the artist.

Police Sergeant Davies

Sergeant Davies headed the small police detachment in Llanidloes. He was a big man in stature, good natured and a natural choice for the role of master of ceremonies when one was required. There was little crime in the town and I rarely heard of any misdemeanours though Valerie, being a Justice of the Peace, would be aware of what happened. If he needed help, Sergeant Davies's approach was direct and usually by telephone. When a new chief constable was appointed to Powys, and stated that all members of his force were to become competent motor cyclists, Sergeant Davies contacted him immediately, and said in effect: "Sir, I wish to be exempted from this requirement as I am much too big to ride a motorbike and would probably fall off." His request was granted, for he was pretty persuasive, and people tended to comply with his wishes. Our practice had no formal affiliation with the police force and none of us was an appointed police surgeon, but that did not deter Sergeant Davies from phoning, as he did on one occasion, and saying: "Doc, John Dee (a teenager) has been caught exposing himself to young girls and the inspector is determined to take him to court. Can you do something about it? The inspector will listen to you." I knew the lad and that he was engaged to get married, so I phoned the inspector who reluctantly agreed not to prosecute if the youth sought psychiatric advice, which he did. That was the end of an incident, dealt successfully by Sergeant Davies.

Two other incidents were potentially more dangerous. They both occurred at night and each was preceded by the usual telephone call. "Doc" the sergeant said, "Mr Jones of Van Terrace is threatening to shoot his wife. Will you go and see him? I will meet you outside the house." So I went, expecting to see Sergeant Davies in Van Terrace, but he was not there and I presumed he was inside. I went in and found the husband and wife alone. Whatever trouble had arisen between them was already settled; he was apologetic and she understanding. Although he had a history of mental illness she was sure he would not hurt her, was concerned and caring for him, and happy that they be left alone together. So I left the house and found Sergeant Davies waiting for me outside. "I knew you would be alright, Doc," he said, before we left for home. Another incident occurred on a moonlit night. The sergeant had contacted me by telephone and asked me to go to Staylittle where a man had gone berserk and was smashing up his home. "A patrol car will be there waiting for you," he said. So I went to Staylittle and, seeing no patrol car, went into the house. Again the situation had been resolved by the time I arrived. This was a younger couple than the folk at Van Terrace and there was no history of mental illness, but he did recognise a tendency in himself to go berserk when the moon was full. All that bad energy had been released by the time I arrived and again the wife was content to be left alone with him. So I left them together and saw a police car waiting outside with two constables sitting in the car looking a bit sheepish. No police action was taken following either incident. Then I was asked to see a younger man who had behaved violently in his mother's house and thrown the television into the street, but had hurt no one. I felt sorry for him. He lived with a mentally tough and very deaf old lady who would have driven me round the bend. Moreover, she would not let the issue rest – she insisted that he was referred for psychiatric advice, or be prosecuted (I cannot remember which), though neither was appropriate. Today a community psychiatric nurse might be asked to visit and assess the situation, but those appointments were yet to come.

Heart Sink Patients

Heart sink patients is a term GPs use to describe chronically sick people with large quantities of medical notes. Medical records are held electronically now, not in hand-written files as formerly. Then each patient had their own separate file and some were very thick, bulging with all sorts of data, mainly reports from hospital doctors. Some reports were quite damning. One was of a man with a husky voice who had attended an ENT consultant for many years and the tone of the letters the consultant wrote were scathing. A typical letter would read: "This man is a dreadful hypochondriac and there is nothing wrong with him." The man saw me again when his usual consultant was away and I sent him to the locum. This time the report was different. He was admitting the patient to hospital with a large cancer of the larynx. It must have been there for years and not seen. As far as I know, the man made no formal complaint and the case was not reviewed by the General Medical Council.

A regular patient was a forestry worker with a large family. I cared for his wife during her last pregnancy, and if I remember rightly, was surprised that the baby's head had some difficulty in emerging. But no intervention was needed and we were all delighted at the birth of her latest child, a son. Six weeks later, I saw the mother and baby in the hospital for her postnatal examination, and the baby's routine assessment. The child's head was noticeably large and he was referred to the paediatric unit at Maelor General Hospital, Wrexham, with a preliminary diagnosis of hydrocephalus, a diagnosis that was confirmed and treated with a shunt. The baby flourished and the parents used to say he was the brightest child in the family. Everyone was pleased with the outcome and the father continued to consult me. Then, suddenly, he stopped coming to the surgery. This interlude lasted many months before he appeared again, but not with his usual complaint. Previously he had always complained about his stomach, as he had a long history of duodenal ulcer and a bulging file that recorded his frequent visits to hospitals. However, this most recent consultation was about something different. Whatever the problem may have been, as he was leaving the surgery he turned round and said: "Doctor, do you remember when I was here last and you gave me a course of antibiotics for my bronchitis? Since then I have had no more trouble with my stomach. I thought you might like to know." He left the surgery and remained a healthy man for the rest of my time at the practice. I thought about his comment very carefully and wondered if I should investigate his remarkable improvement more closely. Should I study the effect amoxicillin might have on other patients in the practice with duodenal ulcers, or just write a letter to the *British Medical Journal* recording my patient's observation and let others look into its therapeutic possibilities? I could see the research potential but did not follow it up, probably because I was very busy and had other research projects that I was pursuing. A few years later, Australian researchers showed that *helicobacter pylori* has a role in causing chronic peptic ulceration and that antibiotics can be curative. The treatment of peptic ulcers is so easy now compared with the past, when partial gastrectomy was a standard treatment for duodenal ulcers. It seems strange that, fifty years ago, I would spend hours in the operating theatre as a student assisting surgeons as they laboured to cure a disease which can now be cured with antibiotics.

Another patient was a farmer who was always the last person to be seen at the end of the surgery on a Saturday night. It was never a brief consultation, he would stay for the best part of half an hour. He always complained of "wind around the heart". In local parlance this meant that he was frightened of having a heart attack. He had been seen by Dr Graham and by Howard Jenkins, our consultant physician, and had had every possible test done, but he continued to appear with great regularity and would question me carefully about his fitness to walk over the hills and care for his sheep. On one occasion I lost my cool and got angry with him, and can remember his hangdog expression as he left the room.

I stopped seeing him for months and thought, good, he has gone to someone else, but then he turned up again with another problem. We managed to resolve this more speedily than usual but, as he was leaving, he turned around and looked at me carefully. He said, "Doctor, do you remember when I was here last, and you told me that there was nothing wrong with me and I could walk over the hills without any problems?" I said yes. He paused and continued: "I went out through that door and stopped. And I thought what a fool I have been." Emphasising his next remark by slapping his hands together, he said: "That was the best bottle of medicine I have ever been given. I go on to the hills now and walk past the townies without any problems at all." He left looking remarkably cheerful and I do not remember seeing him again, but his daughter, who was a teacher in London, always came to see me if she had a medical problem.

Teenage Girls

Trainee GPs tell me that when a young teenager asks to be placed on the contraceptive pill, they are taught to question her carefully before making a decision because of the legal uncertainties that exist. It reminds me of an occasion when three teenagers came to see me at the Castle House surgery for advice. They were not local girls and said they had once attended a family planning clinic for a giggle, but by the time they left the clinic they realised it was not a giggle but an important matter. I have never hesitated to prescribe the pill for teenage girls, including those below the age of consent, but I am totally against the present use of induced abortions as a contraceptive measure and, if an at risk girl had the good sense to seek contraceptive help from me, she got it. These consultations were quite brief: I usually knew the girl and her parents, and a prolonged discussion, or examination, was generally not necessary. As for sexually transmitted diseases, I never saw any. The only infections I saw of the sex organs were vaginal thrush and trichomonas vaginalis, and I believe the same was true for my practice partners. Thirty years later, when I returned to general practice briefly in a different setting, I found that chlamydia infections were quite common.

More time-consuming were teenagers with carpopedal spasm, a painful condition caused by an involuntary contraction of the small muscles of the hands and feet. It is harmless and self-alleviating but can be mistaken for more serious conditions such as a stroke. Within a brief period, I was asked to see three young women with this problem; two are worth mentioning here. The first occurred on a Saturday night when I was asked to go to the home of a St John Ambulance man whom I knew well, and found a young woman writhing on the floor with her hands and feet in spasm. The first-aider thought she was having an epileptic fit but she was conscious, hyperventilating and in carpopedal spasm. Breathing into a paper bag is a recommended treatment because of the hyperventilation, but is not necessary, as the individual usually can be talked into breathing normally and the spasms will then cease. This I did and the young woman soon recovered and was able to tell her story. She was spending a night away from home with a school friend, both were starting their A level examinations on Monday morning, and my patient was also scheduled to give an organ recital at her local chapel on Sunday evening. It was to be her first public performance and, not surprisingly, she was anxious about the outcome. I reassured her and told her that having the carpopedal spasm was a wonderful preparation for the recital, as it enabled her to free herself of any hidden tensions and fears. It augured well for the recital, and similarly she would be particularly well prepared for taking her examinations on Monday. The predictions proved true. The organ recital was a success and she achieved good A level results.

The other incident occurred on a wet autumn evening. There had been a road traffic accident and the ambulance men were dealing with the casualties when I arrived at the scene. They took me immediately into the ambulance to see a young woman who they suspected had serious brain damage. She was conscious, hyperventilating and in carpopedal spasm. I talked to her, and helped to quieten her breathing until the spasm ceased and she was able to sit up and behave normally. We took the casualties to the hospital where I stitched some minor lacerations for a young man. I never saw the young woman again but I think there may have been an interesting sequel. Her father was a professor at Guy's Hospital in London and knew Llanidloes well, and he may have been instrumental in my being offered a senior lecturer post in general practice at Guy's Hospital, even though I had not applied for the post and did not know it was vacant. It was a possible move that needed to be considered carefully, and Val and I visited the general practice department at Guy's but, in the event, I decided not to accept this very prestigious offer, as it would have been a major move for the family at that time.

Hysterical Paralysis

Hysteria was not the common complaint in the late 20th century which it was in Victorian and Edwardian England. The diagnosis is now a rarity and though some people have what is called a 'hysteroid personality', I have seen only one true case of hysteria in almost fifty years of practice. That incident occurred on a Saturday night when I was engaged in a very busy surgery and was least able to do a domiciliary visit. As happened on those occasions, the telephone rang and Miss Parry informed me that there was an urgent call for me to visit a patient at an outlying farmhouse. I spoke to the caller who asked for an immediate visit to his wife, as she was losing the strength in both legs. I explained that the waiting room was full, that many people were wishing to be seen, and that if he could bring his wife to the surgery I would see her immediately. He was doubtful but said he would try. Twenty minutes or so later he phoned again, now from a different house. He had managed to get his wife into the Land Rover and was bringing her to the surgery when her condition worsened and she became totally paralysed. He had stopped at a friend's farmhouse where she was resting, and my immediate presence was required urgently. I was furious. I told the waiting patients of the crisis and went to see the sick lady. At least I did not have to go to the original farmhouse, which was at the end of a steep uneven track that my car could not have traversed. I reached the friend's house where she was temporarily lodged and went in. She was lying on a couch in the sitting room surrounded by worried friends and relatives. She was an attractive young woman and we knew one another quite well, as I had cared for her during her pregnancy and the birth of her daughter, Lowri. She greeted me with the most wonderful smile, and an apparent total acceptance (*belle indifférence*) of her plight. I knew she had a hysteroid tendency and cleared the room of everyone except her and me. She told me she was paralysed and could not move her legs. But I encouraged her to start moving different parts of her lower limbs and slowly with persuasion, she did. Eventually she was able to move her legs quite well whilst lying on the couch, so I got her to sit up with her feet on the floor, then to stand and walk across the room and finally to do a little running on the spot. Having proved she was not paralysed, I left and returned to the patients in my surgery.

It was some weeks, perhaps a month or two later, when I saw her next. This was also a Saturday night, but in Castle House, Tom Brittain's surgery, not in Abernant. I cannot recall the reason for her visit but, as she was leaving, she put a question to me. She was not worried she said, but Lowri had not started to walk and her parents-in-law thought she needed to be seen. What did I think? I told her to bring Lowri to the surgery so I could see her. She did so a week later and when I saw the child, who was about ten months old, I was horrified. Lowri could sit, but she had no strength in her legs and her face was so puffy that she looked like a child on steroids. I referred her to the excellent paediatric unit at the Maelor General Hospital, in Wrexham. There they found that Lowri had a tumour on the adrenal cortex producing the unusual features described. The tumour was removed and the child developed normally. With hindsight, it becomes apparent that the mother's hysterical paralysis was triggered by Lowri's failure to develop normally. Fortunately this was rectified, and both mother and daughter did well.

Less Common Problems

Although I had worked in sub-arctic regions, I had not worked in the tropics and had no experience of tropical medicine. However, I did diagnose one case of malaria in mid Wales. The lady in question had been to East Africa and was working as a physiotherapist in Bronglais Hospital. I saw her twice soon after her return to Wales, both times for a slight feverish illness. On the second occasion I was quite annoyed, as she had driven past my surgery on her way home from Aberystwyth and I was asked to visit her after I had finished my surgery. There was nothing specific about her complaints that I remember, and nothing unusual about her general appearance, but because she had a slight fever and had worked in Kenya I admitted her to the cottage hospital for assessment. We sent blood slides to Bronglais Hospital and asked the laboratory to examine for malaria. The findings were positive and the report stated that the patient had a mild form (ovale) of malaria. She was treated with chloroquine and made a full recovery.

Brucellosis was a disease I enjoyed diagnosing and

treating. It is very debilitating and is easily overlooked but I can recall two cases, both involving young farmers. I probably met the first young man soon after I joined the Llanidloes practice and was asked to visit an elderly farmer who was very ill. When I reached the farmhouse, I found the place in mourning: the man had died and from upstairs I could hear his daughters weeping. Downstairs, his widow was already presiding over a substantial table waiting to receive the friends and relatives who would visit the family and support them in their grief. She looked majestic. In contrast to the tearful sounds coming from above, she appeared to be in complete control of the situation below. Her son was probably a teenager at the time and some years would elapse before he came to the surgery complaining of backache and lassitude. I was not impressed by his complaints, finding nothing wrong with him on physical examination, but I did arrange for the standard tests: chest X-ray, blood profiles and, in his case, for brucella titres. Whilst waiting for the test results, I remember seeing him driving his Land Rover behind a flock of sheep on an otherwise empty country road. He looked worn out, there was no energy in him whatsoever, whilst his two sisters strode cheerfully along the road, one in front of the sheep, the other at the rear. The brucella titre was high and the diagnosis of brucellosis was confirmed. He was treated with tetracycline and his recovery was complete and permanent. The transformation in his appearance was amazing. In some ways it was like diagnosing myxoedema (caused by an underactive thyroid gland), which in its early stages is easily overlooked, but once treatment has begun the change in facial appearance and general health can be great. When treating new cases of myxoedema, I would ask the patient to have a photograph taken before the treatment commenced, and again when better, to illustrate to the family how much the patient's appearance had changed.

The second case of brucellosis involved a man in his early twenties. He came to see me with a painful right shoulder and feeling a bit under the weather. Physical examination revealed nothing unusual and he looked very fit, but I arranged for X-rays of the chest and shoulder and for a standard blood profile but not a brucella titre. When these were reported normal, I referred him to the orthopaedic surgeon who promptly sent him to a rehabilitation centre at a nearby orthopaedic hospital. Whilst he was at the centre, his father came to see me: "Can't something be done for Gareth?" he said. "What do you want me to do Mr Evans?" I replied. He has had his chest and shoulder X-rayed, he has seen a specialist and is now at a rehabilitation centre. What more can I do?" He answered, "Can't you do some tests?" Then the penny dropped. "Send him to me when he comes home from the centre," I said, which he did. His son was feeling a bit better but the shoulder was still painful so I arranged for the laboratory to test him for brucellosis. The titre was high, he was given a course of tetracycline and made a good recovery quite quickly.

Our patients were free to consult any doctor in the practice they chose to see, and we would visit patients of another doctor if asked to do so. The mother of the last baby I delivered at home was one of Tom Brittain's patients. It was his weekend off, and I was in the surgery at Castle House when a farmer's wife telephoned to say her daughter was in great pain and needed an urgent visit. I had just finished the surgery and went immediately. At the farmhouse, the mother took me to see her daughter, who was in her twenties, without realising the nature of the pain. Her daughter was pregnant and in labour. She was not married, having her first baby, and had managed to conceal the pregnancy from the family for nine months. I ordered an ambulance and delivered a full-term baby before the ambulance arrived. Mother and child were then taken to the hospital for a few days rest and assessment. There were no further problems.

Alternative Therapies

I was enjoying a weekend off when Tom Brittain was asked to visit a patient of mine at her home in a farmhouse. She was an elderly woman who I had treated for depression but was complaining of backache on this occasion. Tom gave her some analgesics and advised her to lie flat on her back on the floor. On Monday morning I was asked to see her and found her lying on a flagstone floor in the kitchen. She could not move. I could not leave her in that position, so I talked to her and persuaded her to move a little bit whilst lying on the floor. Eventually she was able to move quite well whilst lying flat, then to sit up, stand and finally walk up the stairs to her bedroom where she could rest more comfortably. I left the house, got into my car and was about to drive away, when the son came out of the house and said, "Doctor, would you wait a moment", and disappeared back into the house. Not knowing what was happening, I waited until he reappeared with something wrapped in newspaper. It was a chunk of meat. He handed the meat to me and said, "Doctor, it is amazing what faith in your doctor will achieve". Then he returned to the house, and I drove away.

I have always been interested in the psychological aspects of medicine and developed an interest in hypnosis whilst I was in the army, where I came across a paper manual on the subject and taught myself some basic skills. But it was a midwife in Llanidloes who encouraged me to practice it as a family doctor. She suggested that I should use it to help women in labour, and I agreed to try. My pregnant mothers liked the idea and a rapid induction into the hypnotic state soon became part of my antenatal care. As I was always present when the baby was born, it suited our routine procedures but I stopped using hypnosis when I realised that some women were such good hypnotic subjects that I might induce a trance inadvertently in situations when it would be inappropriate. Later, when I was at St Mary's Hospice, a nursing sister tried to persuade me to hypnotise her. She wanted to be regressed to her childhood and if possible into her mother's womb, but she was such a willing subject that again I refused to do it.

I got a lot of fun from dowsing my patients with a stethoscope. I learnt about its potential from Andrew Glazewski, a Jesuit priest from Poland, who was the principal speaker at a conference I attended. Entitled 'Passing through the Gateway', it was about our transition into the afterlife, but at the opening session Andrew spoke mainly about developing a sensitivity to physical vibrations, that one can pick up from various sources, such as plants and water and musical instruments. Andrew did not complete his series of lectures, as he died suddenly that first night, but I learnt the essence of what he wished to convey in a brief personal meeting I had with him earlier that evening. There was one other doctor at the conference, a senior cardiologist from St Thomas's Hospital, but I was the doctor who was roused from his bed when Fr Glazewski died. I made no attempt to resuscitate him, because I believed it was the option he would have chosen. It would have been my own choice too if I was in his situation. I learnt hand healing from Andrew but I learnt to dowse from a local dowser who used hazel sticks to detect water. His daughter came to my surgery one day, and I told her that I would like to meet her father. "Oh you want to do that stick thing," she said, "I will ask him." On her next visit to the surgery she confirmed, "he will see you," so I went to his house and learnt how to use dowsing rods to find underground water. I returned home full of enthusiasm, wanting to share my knowledge with my family, but Valerie was not impressed. "I have always known that," she said. Apparently, ever since girlhood, she had been aware of the particular effects that standing close to plants, trees and springs of water can have on the human body. I dowsed patients with my stethoscope because it was not threatening or obtrusive, starting with pregnant women. The patients were generally enthusiastic and content to accept the premise that the body produces fields of energy that can be perceived by the swings of the loosely held stethoscope. Pregnant women were particularly open to the practice, as sexing babies by suspending a needle or wedding ring over a pregnant uterus was a game or custom many had played or knew about. I was surprised by the large swings the stethoscope produced over a near-term uterus and its diminished rotation when the baby was born. Valerie, more of a scientist than I, demanded that the stethoscope should not be held by the human hand, but suspended from a rigid beam before she would accept the authenticity of such tests. She was right, of course, and when the stethoscope was suspended in that way there was no swing over the human body. Later, on becoming interested in spiritual healing, I would hold my hands over Valerie's head, and it always had an effect on her. "That is lovely dear" she would say, "very relaxing".

Manipulative medicine was another interest of mine. It was a technique that Dr Cyriax, a consultant in physical medicine, taught us at St Thomas's Hospital. His father had been a chiropractor and it was mainly chiropractic techniques that he demonstrated to students in the outpatient department. Whilst attendance at OP Clinics was voluntary, there were usually a large number of students present when Dr Cyriax was presiding, and doctors from many parts of the country visited him for relief from their backaches. I am told that some of his books are still read by physiotherapists. Later, when a consultant gave a course of lectures on spinal manipulation at the Sir Robert Jones and Agnes Hunt Orthopaedic Hospital in Oswestry, I attended them. He was an orthopaedic surgeon and an osteopath and, having learnt some of his skills, I used his methods instead of the more vigorous manipulations of Dr Cyriax. I had enough success with spinal manipulation to try it on my wife, and we were both surprised by my freeing her instantly of a painful back. It is one of the few occasions when I considered the treatment that I had given Valerie to be helpful. She was rarely ill and then usually consulted other doctors.

Folk medicine

My maternal grandfather was a self-sufficient man. He built his own water mill and was his own healer, not bothering with doctors but finding his own medicines in the fields and gardens of his neighbourhood. He died of pneumonia in his fifties, before antibiotics were available to save him. Rural areas had many alternative healers before modern medicine dominated the therapeutic scene. In mid Wales the more skilled healers were called conjurors, as in Shakespeare's England, and accounts of their practices and their roles in the community were still related when I was in Llanidloes. The best known was Morris of the Vulcan Arms in Cwmbelan, the hamlet where Graham Davies had extracted a fighter pilot from his crashed plane. Morris was still practising in the 1940s, and I had a long chat with a lady who remembered him visiting the family farm when she was a child. She said her mother took him into the sitting room, not to the kitchen where most people went, and left him there, alone. Being an inquisitive girl she crept up to the door, peered through the keyhole and saw Morris sitting at the table, writing. Her mother caught her spying and scolded her, but when Morris left she saw him hand a slip of paper to her mother, who placed it in a stone wall at the front of the house. Years later, the wall collapsed and, at the spot where her mother had posted the paper, she found a bottle containing several pieces of paper. They were magical prescriptions for the healing of sick animals, and people on the farm. Conjurors were respected men and their advice on the management of common illnesses was often sought.

Morris lived at the Vulcan Arms, where he worked as a blacksmith. People used to meet at his smithy to chat, and whilst the conversation centred around local interests, Morris was also knowledgeable about poetry, astronomy and natural history. In his role as a conjuror, he consulted a book on magic which he left to the National Library of Wales at Aberystwyth. It is now held in the manuscript department of the library and is entitled 'The Art of Talismanic Magic. Being Selections from the Works of Rabbi Solomon, Agrippa, Barrett etc.' and is dated 1888.[17] It begins by telling the aspirant to live a disciplined and virtuous life, and ends with the admonition:

> Whoever attempts to understand the Great Mysteries.
> Let him live up to the teachings of Jesus Christ.
> His Redeemer and Saviour.
> Who died for the sins of all.

There seems to have been little conflict of interest between the conjurors and the local medical practitioners. The former were consulted mainly for everyday concerns about health, the latter more frequently for matters of life and death. According to Robert Gibbings, an Irish academic who knew Morris, "the real point about the conjuror is that he was wise".[18] Gibbings also visited another local conjuror, George Lloyd, to seek relief for his persistent backache. They met in the back kitchen of a farmhouse and chatted about various things before the subject of Gibbings' pain was raised. Then Lloyd said he would heal him and did so by winding a ball of wool around his arm, and then attaching some thread to Gibbing's leg. Lloyd predicted the pain would disappear completely in a week. It did so and never returned.[19]

Research in General Practice

I made my first attempt to write an original paper a few weeks before flying to Labrador. The College of General

Practitioners had offered a prize for an essay entitled 'Second Opinions' and, because the subject was intriguing, I entered the competition. Having written my contribution in long hand, I sent it to the retired naval officer in charge of the college's administration, then departed for Labrador. Some months later I received a letter from the lieutenant commander reporting that the essay had not been assessed as it had arrived one day after the scheduled date. I was very upset. Later in Llanidloes, I had the good fortune to have my first attempt at research accepted and published by the *British Medical Journal*; it was a paper entitled 'A Pregnant Woman Struck by Lightning'. Seeing the paper in print was a huge boost to my self-confidence, and had the BMJ rejected it I would probably not have attempted any further research.

A previous section mentions my paper on 'Agriculture Tractor Accidents'. In the 1960s I thought this might provide a suitable subject for the MD (Doctor of Medicine) degree, which relatively few general practitioners then held, but I did not know any GPs with an MD who could advise on the process, and there were various administrative obstacles that needed to be overcome. For instance, my own university (London) required that a general practitioner be qualified for seven years before enrolling for the exam: doctors at approved hospitals could take the exam after four years. Another requirement stated that doctors aiming for an MD should first seek help and advice from a recognised university teacher. This was a major obstacle as I had a research project in mind, but no contact with university teachers for taking it further. Then Professor Davies, my old professor of anatomy at St Thomas's, walked into the surgery with teaching aids for Graham to use in instructing St John Ambulance men. I hadn't appreciated that the professor had a connection with the practice, but it transpired that his father had bought a house in Llanidloes and was a patient of Graham's. I took the opportunity to discuss the situation with him and he was both helpful and optimistic, suggesting that I contact the dean's office, which would arrange for a suitable teacher to help. Soon I received a letter from the medical school naming a senior lecturer who had been asked to advise me. I knew the man and was disappointed because I was aware that he had no experience of general practice or the subject of my thesis. On receiving a letter from him requesting details of my proposed thesis, I replied with some arrogance, and retribution followed swiftly. He indicated that I would be wasting my time attempting an MD, but could discuss the matter with him in person if I wished. I duly went to London, and recall three things about the visit. On the train I read Pope John XXIII's autobiography, *Journal of a Soul*, an excellent book for increasing humility, but not the best preparation for arguing the merits of a proposed thesis. My second recollection is of the little importance he gave to our meeting, arriving very late, having been delayed by "an important committee meeting". My third and most vivid memory was not so much the reaffirmation that I would be wasting my time pursuing an MD degree, but of being told that the failure rate was 95 per cent, which I knew was not true. I left like the metaphorical dog with my tail between my legs, but became increasingly annoyed on considering the matter. I therefore wrote to the medical secretary asking for a different adviser, someone with an interest in rural accidents and experience in general practice, and received the type of reply a cooler mind might have expected. In polite words I was told to go to hell and that it would be useless to seek advice elsewhere.

Stung by this, I re-read the university regulations governing the MD degree and found that, although candidates were required to obtain the advice of a recognised teacher, it did not stipulate that the advice be accepted. I therefore decided to proceed with my project and write an MD thesis unaided. Eventually, I submitted the work to the university with the requisite fee and application form, dealing with the clause requiring the name of the approved university teacher by giving the name of my erstwhile adviser, stating that his advice was not to attempt the thesis. The university reacted remarkably well. Although only the letter of the regulations had been observed, the thesis was read and I was invited to a viva voce. The courtesy of the examining panel and the charm of its chairman was such that I returned home with reasonable hopes of success. The subsequent letter of regret, though disappointing, left me feeling that the university had looked fairly at my thesis and had quite properly failed me. That the research undertaken for the thesis resulted in two original articles in the *British Medical Journal* and two articles in less esteemed journals, was some consolation. My 'Agricultural Tractor Accidents' was one published paper, and the British Medical Association awarded me its Sir Charles Hastings Prize for a second, published by the *British Medical Journal* in 1967.[20] With the prize money, I bought myself a typewriter.

It was not my intention to try again, but a collaborative paper published with Sylvia Lutkins in 1967 on 'Mortality of Bereavement'[21] probably contained enough good material for an MD thesis. It showed that bereavement is associated with an increased mortality, particularly in men, and is still cited, but I thought what is the use of an MD in general practice anyway? The answer was not much, as the possession of an MD was of no real value for a GP in the 1960s. It made no difference to his income, or the work he did, and added nothing to his status vis-à-vis his colleagues. So why did I try again? Quite frankly it was not to obtain an MD per se, but to obtain academic approval for my next research project. I realised that the subject matter was so unusual that it might not be taken seriously. After publishing the 'Mortality of Bereavement', I began a longitudinal study of the physical and mental effects of bereavement, exploring such aspects as weight loss, insomnia and depression. I soon found that a large proportion of people interviewed were telling me about, what they considered to be, true perceptions of dead relatives. This finding so intrigued me that I decided to look into it further, though restricting the survey to widowed people. Consultation with my colleagues, and local clergy, showed them to be as little aware of this widespread phenomenon as I had been. A literature search showed that almost no scientific data had been recorded on this subject, and the textbooks of medicine contained no mention of it at all. So I abandoned my longitudinal survey in favour of this new interest. The findings are recorded in my MD thesis 'The Hallucinatory Reactions of Bereavement', and in a paper 'The Hallucinations of Widowhood' published in 1971 in the BMJ.[22]

Now that I was again interested in writing an MD thesis, I needed to obtain the advice of a recognised university teacher. Unwilling to face another rebuff from my medical school, I wrote to the university registrar. By reply came a letter advising me strongly to try the medical school again. So I swallowed my pride and wrote to the dean. This time the pattern was different. On my side I was much more careful and impersonal than previously in presenting my proposed project. As a consequence, the assigned adviser proved sympathetic and knowledgeable. He was a senior psychiatrist and was prepared to spend a great deal of time helping me. Two things became clear at our constructive initial meeting. Firstly, the project outlined was certainly worth a Ph.D. but possibly did not contain enough clinical data to merit an MD. I was advised to extend the scope of my thesis and duly did so. Secondly it transpired that I could not register for the MD within the discipline of general practice, as there were no academic departments of general practice at the university, so the degree would be registered as research in the field of psychiatry. On his advice too I visited Cardiff to discuss the project with Professor Rawnsley, another psychiatrist, and made a similar journey to the Royal College of General Practitioners' research and statistical unit at Birmingham.

Both journeys were well worthwhile, and I remain grateful for the advice and help provided.

Writing a thesis while fully engaged in a busy rural practice did not allow time for developing elegant prose, but when the work was complete I was content. My labours had not yet finished, however; three more tasks needed to be completed. The first was to speak about my work to psychiatrists at the Royal Society of Medicine, which I did. The second was to find four academic psychiatrists who would read and criticise the thesis before I could submit it to the university, and again I am grateful to the two professors and the two consultants who accepted such a tedious chore. One reader, Professor Hinton, considered that the contents were good but that the presentation was inadequate and the format too tedious for the examiners. He advised a rewrite of the thesis, which I undertook and felt was worth the extra effort. The final hurdle was to attend an international conference of psychiatrists where I was the only GP to address the meeting. The paper was well received by the delegates and, on the same day, a paper based on my thesis was published in the BMJ. On the Monday I learnt that I had been awarded the MD.

My piece at the conference was given on a Friday and the next day, several national newspapers carried reports of the research. The work was also described in the Sunday papers. More importantly, the findings were not disputed but accepted by the medical profession and replicated in other centres, notably in the USA. The study has altered our understanding of the frequency with which people experience what some may call contact with their dead husband or wife. It showed that almost 50 per cent of widowed people experience some sense of their spouse in moments of clear consciousness. These experiences can include not just a sense of the dead person's presence, but visual perceptions also, and even a sense of being touched or hugged. This is accepted as being a normal, helpful and common experience of widowhood now and, contrary to Freudian teaching, does not hinder the grief process but can facilitate it. They do not affect overt behaviour and tend to disappear with time, though they sometimes persist for many years. People are able to integrate the experience and keep it secret, even from a new spouse if the person has remarried. Most importantly, the incidence does not vary with social variants such as gender, education, race, domicile and other similar factors.

Overall, my research interests as a general practitioner, and later as Medical Director of St Mary's Hospice, covered rural accidents, bereavement, the distress of dying, the health of motorists, postnatal depression, the role of the hospices in terminal care and the use of opioid drugs in palliative medicine. A full list of my publications is given in the Appendix. This is included, partly because the reader may wish to have the information, but also because the scope for GPs developing scientific studies of patterns observed in their work should be outlined and, to some limited extent, substantiated. This latter reason is discussed further in the final section of this book.

One last thought. People who do research are often asked to speak at conferences or meetings and I have given my fair share of such lectures. The occasion that stands out most clearly in my memory was being asked to speak on 'The Domiciliary Care of the Terminally Ill' at the University Hospital Cardiff, where the principal speaker was Cicely Saunders, the founder of the hospice movement and a most charismatic public speaker. The morning session was apportioned in 20 minute slots to consultants from the Cardiff teaching hospitals. Only two speakers were scheduled for the afternoon session; both were given an hour. Cicely Saunders had the opening session and mine was the concluding one. As a GP from rural Wales, the problem of following Cicely was daunting. Then I remembered that she always showed slides of patients she cared for at St Christopher's Hospice. They all looked splendid. So I followed her lead and hired a professional photographer to film my patients in their own homes. The first person approached was a tough old lady with breast cancer who lived in an isolated house by herself and had, on one occasion, driven herself to my surgery with a fractured wrist. When we reached the house, she came to the door looking dishevelled. I explained about the conference and asked if we could take her photograph. She considered for a moment, then said, "Come back in half an hour", which we did. The transformation was great, she looked smashing. On the day of the conference, the lecture hall was packed, and even my contribution went down well.

People often ask me why I left Llanidloes. It is a difficult question to answer. I had no reason to leave and it was the happiest phase of my professional career, but I always knew (inwardly) that my tenure would be limited. Possibly, if I had taken longer holidays, and been more relaxed in my life and work, I would have stayed, but sometimes I would get itchy feet and look at other possibilities. The offer of a senior lecturer post at Guy's Hospital was unsettling, and the partners had arranged to move into a purpose-built unit which made my departure simpler as Abernant would no longer be needed as a practice house. Also my family expressed no dissent, so when a prestigious job with the Civil Service Department became available, I applied for it and, to my surprise, was appointed. When I left, the partnership invited my friend, Tuppin Scrase, to replace me. Before we met, Tuppin was a research registrar in anaesthetics, and was considering moving into general practice, but needed some practical experience before making a decision. A mutual friend contacted me and asked if I could help, which I was happy to do. Valerie was in agreement, so Tuppin and his wife Andy (also a doctor) spent a week with us at Abernant, and we became good friends. They liked what they saw of the practice and area, and Tuppin decided to train as a GP in northern England. The completion of Tuppin's training in general practice coincided with my departure from Llanidloes, and so he applied for and was appointed to the post.

6

The Civil Service
Department 1974–6

Enborne

WE LEFT LLANIDLOES in 1973 and found a temporary home
at Enborne, near Newbury, in Berkshire. There we rented
a modern rectory, with a large garden that overlooked the
Enborne, a stream made famous by the novelist Richard
Adams in his book *Watership Down*. Enborne was the starting
point for Adams' story of a band of wild rabbits that journeyed
from a doomed warren at Enborne to the relative safety of a
distant hill called Watership Down. Richard Adams was a civil
servant and, like him, in my new role with the Civil Service
Department, I travelled by train from Newbury to Paddington
Station and thence to the office in London. Mine was at Petty
France in central London where I had a splendid oak panelled
room that overlooked the guards' barracks and St James' Park.
Later I moved up a flight where I had an even better view of
the park and could still hear the regimental bands practising
in the barracks below. As a leaving present, I had been given a
cheque by the staff at Llanidloes Hospital and used the money
to buy a bicycle which I rode from the station to the office, but
only for five days a week as I no longer worked at weekends. I
found a convenient place, behind the church of St James the
Great in Paddington, where I could chain the bike to railings
at the end of each working day and collect it in the mornings.
Then I would cycle across Hyde Park, down Constitution Hill

to Buckingham Palace and into Petty France, dodging the traffic en route.

Valerie chose the house at Enborne. I think she was happy there. She enjoyed the solitude and rural location, and became an active member of the local riding for the disabled group. After a brief spell of uncertainty, David settled happily into his new school at Newbury, riding his bicycle along steep and narrow roads, on his way home. Anna was at Millfield School in Somerset and Eileen at Leicester University, where she seemed to spend most of her time mountaineering at weekends rather than focussing on her studies. Two of the family's ponies, Brandy and Copper, came to Newbury with us and soon settled in a nearby field. During their school holidays, Anna and her future husband Marc, rode them along the gallops at Lambourn, which was known locally as the valley of the horses because so many racehorses were bred and trained there. The old mare Arrow, from which we bred Brandy and Copper, was sold with help from our friends Dick and Lavinia Vaughan of Gorn Farm, and stayed in Llanidloes.

The Medical Adviser's Office

The Civil Service Department was an elite branch of the Civil Service. It was established by the Harold Wilson Government in 1968 to support the personnel employed by the Civil Service, and most of its original members came from the Treasury. As a senior medical officer in the medical adviser's office, I was invited to a private meeting with the head of the Civil Service Department, at that time Sir William Armstrong, which took place in his office in central London, close to ours in Petty France. The head of the medical service was Sir Daniel Thomson, who had played an important role in establishing the Salk Vaccine programme against poliomyelitis in the UK, and seven other doctors were employed by the service – all had higher degrees. One was a former professor of medicine and the others had been high ranking medical officers in the armed forces. We had three nurses, and various supporting staff who worked mainly as personal assistants and typists.

Whitehall 2 Study

One thing that attracted me to the Civil Service Department was the opportunity it provided for involvement with a large-scale research project. Whilst I was there I took part in the Whitehall 2 Study, which involved monitoring the health of over 10,000 civil servants based in London, and was established following the success of the earlier Whitehall 1 Study, initiated in 1967. A long-term follow-up of the two studies is still ongoing and various papers have been published on the findings. The most important result was finding a strong association between people's status in the Civil Service and their death rates from a range of causes. Thus the mortality rate for people in the lower grades of employment – messengers, doorkeepers, etc. – is three times higher for cardiovascular disease than among people in the highest (administrator) grades of the Civil Service.

During my time in the service, we collected baseline data that included a self-reported questionnaire, a chest X-ray, blood pressure, electrocardiogram, and a range of blood tests including blood sugar and thyroid function tests. The bloods were sent to Birmingham for analysis but, apart from the X-ray which was taken by a radiographer on site, the other data was collected by the nurses at Petty France. Each individual was also examined by a doctor. All the tests were collected on the same day, which contrasts favourably with the current 21st century situation in general practice, where a routine assessment of blood pressure, blood profiles and urine can require three visits to the surgery without seeing a doctor. In Whitehall I spent two half-days each week conducting the clinical examinations, seeing six men each afternoon. The sessions were intentionally leisurely, and a surprisingly large proportion of men said: "I have never had such a thorough examination before." I was also one of the doctors who coded the electrocardiograms, using the 'Minnesota code' so that the results could be recorded electronically.

Cardiology at St Thomas's

To maintain the high standards required by the Civil Service Department, each doctor spent a half-day each week at a centre of clinical excellence. I asked to be attached to the department of general practice at St Thomas's Hospital but Sir Daniel considered that inadequate for the work we did. Instead, I arranged with Dr Webb-Peploe, the senior cardiologist at St Thomas's, to spend a morning each week at his clinic and eventually became quite adept at detecting unusual heart murmurs. It was there that I first saw an echocardiogram (then still a new technique) in use, and a coronary angioplasty performed for the first time. The patient was a well-built policeman and the team set about its business expertly. Suddenly his heart stopped beating, the alarm was raised and a resuscitation team rushed into the theatre and restored his heart to its normal rhythm. The delay in conducting the angioplasty was brief, and the procedure continued as though nothing unusual had happened. I witnessed my next coronary angioplasty twenty-five years later at the Walsgrave Hospital in Coventry, where I was the patient being treated. I observed the procedure on an overhead screen, and left the Walsgrave Hospital with the first of three stents which were eventually placed in my coronary arteries.

The British Museum

My main task was to oversee the health of civil servants employed by the Ministry of Defence (MoD) and by the London museums. Routine problems were dealt with in my office; others required an on-site assessment. On one occasion I was asked to assess the high incidence of coronary thrombosis that was reported in a specialised department of the British Museum. This department, which was located not in the main building in Bloomsbury but in the East End of London, was responsible for ensuring that any items that were sent to the museum for display were in perfect condition when exhibited, and my visit coincided with the museum's preparation for an important exhibition of Islamic art in the Hayward Gallery. Most of the exhibits had just arrived from the Middle East and were awaiting assessment, and possible repair, by the British Museum's skilled artists and craftsmen. I expected everything to be neat and tidy, but on entering the building was confronted by a large pile of unsorted exhibits lying on the floor, waiting to be fumigated. It seemed a motley collection that did not merit inclusion in a major exhibition in London, but I walked around the mound with interest and went upstairs to discuss medical matters with the civil servants. When eventually the exhibition of Islamic art went on display to the public, it looked magnificent – in no way comparable with the mixed and varied pile of items that I had seen on the floor of the repair shop. As I proceeded round the Hayward Gallery, I touched some of the exhibits, now beautifully displayed on the walls and stands. An attendant immediately approached me and said: "Sir, please don't touch sir, it is not allowed." I said nothing, but smiled inwardly at the differing attitude given to this amazing collection in the two locations where I was privileged to view it.

A Friend's Son

Much of the routine work for the MoD was given to assessing the appropriateness of allowing civilian employees to be discharged from the service on medical grounds. Medical discharge carried considerable financial benefits to the individual but increased costs to the Government and taxpayer. I remember just a few of these cases. The most memorable was a young principal who had been a university lecturer before joining the Ministry of Defence. His father had an excellent record in World War II and was highly regarded as a senior member of the MoD, so his son was expected to be equally able. He wasn't, at least in this field. He was a pleasant young man of good intelligence, but his father was of exceptional character and had particular ability getting on with senior members of the armed forces. The son's seniors decided that he was over-promoted and should step down a rank from principal to higher executive officer. He refused to comply and his head of department, wishing to be rid of him, decided to seek his dismissal on medical grounds. His case came to me. We met in my office, he remained adamant that he would not go, and I was equally determined not to discharge him unless he was content to do so. Eventually he did agree and left the service with a useful pension. Normally I would have lost track of him completely, but when I returned to general practice and became settled as a GP in Warwickshire, my wife and I were invited to tea by a married couple who were patients of mine. They were a charming pair who had been married for many years. The husband had been a senior member of the MoD and they had one son and a daughter. At this first social meeting they naturally talked about their children and we learnt that their son, who had also been in the MoD, had left early to establish a successful school for crammers in a university town where he had died quite suddenly and unexpectedly. On listening to the story, it became apparent that the son was the young principal whom I had known in London and discharged on medical grounds. I was pleased that I had not forced him to retire but had waited until he was ready to do so. I never mentioned this association to the parents, but wonder if they sometimes thought that I might have been involved with their son leaving the Civil Service. We remained good friends and, when the father, then a widower moved to the north of England, we continued to correspond until he died.

The Icelandic Cod Wars

Whilst I was associated with the MoD, the Icelandic Cod Wars became increasingly confrontational. This series of incidents, regarding fishing rights in the north Atlantic, escalated in 1972 when Iceland unilaterally declared an Exclusive Economic Zone and extended its fisheries limits from 12 to 50 nautical miles. It used its coastguards to police the extended area and this led to various net-cutting incidents and several cases of Icelandic and British vessels ramming each other. Royal Navy warships were sent to protect the British fishermen in the area and diplomatic relations became very tense. The dispute was settled in 1976 when Britain backed down. I do not think shots were fired by the British but it might have come to that and the pressure on diplomats must have been considerable. Whether the Cod Wars were a factor in my being called to the Foreign Office is uncertain, but I was certainly summoned when a minister involved in the dispute collapsed in his office and required medical help. The sense of crisis was so great that I was taken to see him in a ministry car, but from the medical perspective his problem was not major and was readily alleviated.

Leprosy in London

One of the more unusual clinical cases seen at Petty France, a woman with leprosy was perhaps the most interesting. A colleague came to my office with a young woman, and asked me to look at a lesion on her hand. It was obviously a trick question as he wanted to show me an interesting case and to see if I could make a correct diagnosis. The patient looked very fit and had no complaints except for a large white blemish, of fairly recent onset, on the back of her hand. She had no pain and there was no sensation in the affected area. She had lived in the Middle East and the stitch marks of a recent biopsy were evident in the skin. My friend Terry was surprised when I said she had leprosy. It was a nice case to see and also nice to make a correct diagnosis. It wasn't clear how she had acquired the disease as skin-skin contact is now considered to be an unlikely route of infection, but in order to be seen by a doctor at Petty France, she would probably have worked overseas for a Government department. There are various forms of leprosy, and the nature of her lesion was typical of Tuberculoid leprosy, the most benign form of the disease. Though this type of leprosy is often self-limiting, she would have been treated for six months with a combination of the drugs rifampicin and dapsone.

Homeopathy and Osteopathy

Compared with general practice, life as a civil servant was comparatively easy. Travelling to and from work took about two hours on the train, but I had standard holidays, all my weekends free, and could organise my own time and work schedules. At lunch time, I could cycle to the Tate Gallery where the sandwiches were excellent, loll in St James's Park, attend a lunchtime concert in the church at Smith's Square or swim in the indoor pool at Pimlico. All these things I enjoyed, but managed to observe other things too. A school of osteopathy was based within a short walk of the office and I asked if it might be possible to attend some of the lectures. Perhaps because I was a doctor, I was made welcome, and despite attending only a few sessions found these quite fascinating. The manner in which the teachers and students approached their patients was much more sensitive and friendly than is normally seen on medical wards, and I was also impressed by the gentleness with which they touched the patients. I liked the ambience of the place a lot and would have liked to have been able to spend more time there.

The Royal Homeopathic Hospital was another place that I enjoyed visiting, this time to gain a better insight into the practice of homeopathy. There again I felt welcomed and at ease and, on explaining my intentions, was taken to a consulting room where a doctor was busy with patients. We chatted for a while and during the conversation he explained they were short of staff that day and asked if I would take a clinic for him. I said yes, and suddenly found myself seeing patients who regarded me as a homeopathic consultant, which I found to be a novel but pleasant experience. One group I saw was an Asian family, a mother with young children, of whom one had asthma. The child had been referred by her GP to the Hammersmith Hospital, where she had been seen and prescribed conventional medicine. However, the mother had not given the medicine to her daughter. Instead she brought both medicine and child to the Homeopathic Hospital to make sure that the treatment was suitable. I assured her that it was and the family went away with, I hope, sufficient reassurance to use it, confident that it would benefit rather than be harmful to the child.

Returning to General Practice

Although I enjoyed the leisurely life of being a civil servant, I knew at heart it was not my sphere. I was more of a hands-on doctor, and there were also financial problems that needed to be resolved. This was the period of the Callaghan Government when inflation was escalating, and we no longer owned a house of our own. My salary was excellent but I knew that I could earn more money as a GP in a dispensing practice. So I spoke to Sir Daniel and told him that I was looking for a new post. He understood and eventually I was offered a single-handed dispensing practice in the heart of England, in leafy Warwickshire. Before moving, I did one other job in London, a week's locum as a senior house officer in neurology at the Whittington Hospital, mainly because

I felt the need to have a better understanding of this field. The medical registrar, who made the appointment, said he chose me because he was intrigued by my CV and wanted to know why a senior doctor should be interested in such a junior post. I remember little about the Whittington Hospital except for cutting a man's toenails, a retired actor who had an important role in the early TV series of *Dr Who*. By the time I saw him he was quite old and no longer able to reach his nails, which were so long that walking was difficult. No one in the hospital was prepared or allowed to do it, so I trimmed his nails which pleased him, and he was able to walk more easily afterwards. In 1981, the Margaret Thatcher Government decided that the Civil Service Department was not cost-effective and its specific role should be reallocated to other departments. The department was closed and its functions went mainly to the Cabinet Office.

7

Rural Warwickshire
1976–80

Dr Peter Robert McElwain (1916–76)

I RETURNED TO general practice as a sole practitioner at Stretton-on-Dunsmore, a village in the heart of England. The towns of Coventry, Leamington Spa and Rugby are within eight miles of the village, whilst Birmingham, Oxford and Stratford-upon-Avon are conveniently close. The practice was established after World War II by Dr Peter Robert McElwain, an Irishman known locally as Bob Mac. Little is known of Bob Mac's roots except that he went to boarding school and medical school in Ireland, and then joined the RAF Medical Service probably during World War II. He returned to civilian life in the late 1940s to early 1950s, when he bought a large terrace house in Leamington Spa, set up his plate and started a new practice. At first he had few patients, but he extended the practice area to include Princethorpe, which had a well-established Roman Catholic community, and the villages of Marton and Stretton-on-Dunsmore. In Marton, patients consulted him in an old schoolroom, whilst in Stretton-on-Dunsmore, he rented a room in the village hall. Slowly the practice grew, as the people in Princethorpe and the surrounding communities came to know and like him. Eventually he needed a more convenient base than his house in Leamington Spa, so he bought a plot of land in Stretton-on-Dunsmore and applied to the local authority for permission to build a house and surgery. Although the plot was in a green belt area, the provision of a surgery resulted in his being given planning consent to build in a village that had existed for many centuries. He was a popular doctor and ran the practice with just one assistant, Miriam Mitchell, who was both his receptionist and dispenser. Miriam describes Bob as "being great for a laugh, a swear and a curse". He could be irascible, and one night when he was woken by a man with a minor injury, he sent him away in no uncertain terms, telling Miriam "all he wanted was a bloody sick note". His was a dispensing practice with branch surgeries in Marton and in the village hall at Ryton-on-Dunsmore. Eventually, he became medical officer to Princethorpe College, then a Catholic day and boarding school, and to the Police Training Centre at Ryton. This latter appointment provided him with a stream of temporary residents, the numbers amounting to a few hundred each year. In addition he delivered babies at home and joined the Rugby Medical Group, a team of local doctors who provided instant medical cover whenever a road traffic accident occurred in their vicinity. He died aged 60 from cancer of the colon, leaving his widow Kate to cope alone with four children of school age who were all attending fee-paying schools. Because he was a self-employed doctor with no partners, Kate was responsible for finding the locums needed to maintain the practice following his death, though in this she would have been helped by the Family Practitioner Committee (FPC).

Bob Mac died in 1976. When the funeral cortege passed through the village for his requiem mass at Princethorpe Priory Church, people lined the street and the men doffed their hats as a sign of respect. Few doctors would be honoured in that way now. The FPC suggested uniting the practice with a neighbouring practice, but the people of Stretton were strongly opposed to such a move, and because Kate was willing to rent the surgery premises in her house, a vacancy was advertised in the medical press. I was interviewed and appointed for the post. Under the Callaghan Government, house prices had escalated and there were no houses for sale in the neighbourhood, so it took several months to relocate my family from Newbury. Luckily Miriam, and her husband John, were prepared to rent me a room and look after me during the interim period. I was with them for almost a year and we became, and remain very good friends. Meanwhile, Val and David stayed at Enborne which suited David because he was happy at his school and was unenthusiastic about moving. My return to general practice was based in a house that was in mourning, so I made no adjustments to the routines that Bob Mac had established. Most crucially I did not introduce an appointment system, though some patients would have welcomed it, and Miriam continued in her role as receptionist and dispenser. Kate and Miriam were good friends, providing support for one another, and naturally I saw a lot of Kate during those early months. She needed to talk and I spent long sessions in her sitting room listening as she talked about Bob and her current problems. Slowly, I took over the non-NHS activities that Bob Mac had undertaken at the Police Training Centre and Princethorpe College. Both were remunerative and supportive of me as the incoming doctor. Princethorpe even gave me a salary, additional to the NHS fees I received for the boys at the school, and provided me with a rent-free house when my family moved to Warwickshire.

Police Training Centre

My association with the Police Training Centre continued seamlessly from Bob Mac's days. Most mornings, a minibus from the training centre brought sick or injured police personnel to the surgery, and there were usually one or more police officers or recruits in the waiting room. Miriam oversaw the arrivals and dispensed the drugs. She also acted as my chaperone. It was a friendly and efficient system as

Miriam knew most of the patients well, having lived in the area all her life. The nature of the waiting area is nicely depicted in a cartoon that a patient drew and gave to me on leaving. Local characters can be recognised from the drawing, and though people appear huddled together, the cartoon portrays the general mood of good humour that prevailed there. As one old patient said to me recently, "it was a cosy place". A short passage separated the waiting and consulting rooms which helped to ensure the patients' privacy during our consultations. Unfortunately, I cannot remember the artist's name though the cartoon is signed M L.

On two mornings each week, I went to the Police Training Centre to give a lecture to the recruits. Most were young men and women but a few were older people who had served in the army and had some experience of injuries and first aid. It was Bob Mac's custom to deliver the same series of lectures almost verbatim, without altering one word in the lecture he had prepared, but that would have bored me stiff. The prospect of standing for an hour talking to rows of uninspired faces was too daunting, so whilst the topic at each session was determined by the requirements of the course, I always varied my method of delivering it. For instance, if the subject was emergency childbirth, I would start by asking if anyone had ever been in a situation where they had to deliver a baby. Sometimes an older recruit would raise a hand and say yes, and I would ask him (in those days it was usually a man) to tell the class of his experience. The response that became immediately apparent was the intense interest with which the other recruits listened to the narrator speak, and I was always fascinated by the sense of privilege the men felt at having helped to deliver a baby.

Initially there were about thirty recruits in each new intake, but the numbers at the centre increased rapidly with a reorganisation of the police training service in the 1970s. Some training centres were closed but the

Ryton-on-Dunsmore centre was expanded and renamed. Eventually I was asked if I would teach two sets of recruits simultaneously, to which I said yes, and later if I would accept a third set (90 recruits) simultaneously in each session. Again I said yes, though I doubt if my lecture fee was increased. I was the only speaker at these lectures, but a police sergeant who had been at the centre for some years taught other parts of the first aid course and was the first person recruits consulted if they felt ill. He left the training centre at the same time as myself, and whilst our recruits had a 100 per cent pass rate for the first aid exams, this fell, at least for a while, to 70 per cent when we left and new instructors were appointed. Other changes have occurred since then, and I believe the medical care and training is now provided mainly by a nurse employed by the Police Training Centre.

Princethorpe College

I enjoyed being the medical officer at Princethorpe College. The school was founded in the late 1950s by Irish priests of the MSC (Missionaries of the Sacred Heart) congregation who were very kind to me. Established originally in Royal Leamington Spa, the school moved to Princethorpe in 1966, where it occupies a former Benedictine convent surrounded by 200 acres of parkland. Its chapel and gatehouses were designed by Pugin. In my time, Princethorpe College was an independent boarding and day school for boys only; now it is a mixed gender school and accepts day pupils only. The school has flourished and currently has about 800 pupils who are bussed in from the surrounding towns and villages. I was appointed the school's medical officer by the then headmaster, Fr Clarkson, when the boarding contingent was quite large and included pupils from China and Africa. The college had MSC priests on the teaching staff in the late 1970s, but Fr Ted is the only priest still there, being both school chaplain and parish priest for the local Catholic community. I used to visit the school each Tuesday afternoon to hold a weekly surgery for the boys. Sr Marie, the matron, was very efficient and always had tea and biscuits waiting for me when the surgery was finished. I can recall just one medical crisis that occurred at the school. It happened one evening when Sr Marie asked me to see a young teenager who was in great pain. He is the only person I have ever seen with a torsion of the testicle, and to relieve the intense pain I gave him an injection of pethidine before admitting him to St Cross Hospital in Rugby. When I phoned the surgical registrar the next morning he seemed very cool about the admission. Apparently when the lad arrived at St Cross, the pain had gone and the torsion had rectified itself. At least my treatment was effective and the boy did not require the immediate surgery that I had expected.

One thing that Fr Clarkson required of me when I joined the staff was to assess the public health needs of the school and, in particular, to prepare a detailed report on the state of the kitchens and food hygiene. With 200 acres of parkland, the school had its own farm and herd of dairy cattle and prided itself on providing fresh milk each day to the pupils. Unfortunately, the milk was not pasteurised and the herd was not tuberculin tested. Consequently the milk was a potential hazard to the well-being of the boys and my report pointed to the danger of using untreated milk. The school's response was surprisingly quick. It sold its herd of cattle and obtained its milk from another source.

Cross Roads Care

Noel Crane was one of my more interesting patients. He was a paraplegic who lived in a bungalow in Marton and was cared for by his elderly mother. She washed him, dressed him and each morning sent him to work in his disabled person's car. Noel was in his middle years when I knew him, and it was always a joy to visit the house, but I had to be careful not to drink much of the scrumpy (a very strong West Country cider) they sometimes offered me. Noel's paraplegia was the result of an accident in north Wales, where he had gone swimming, and had dived into a stretch of water that was not very deep, breaking his neck. He survived the immediate impact of the accident and was transferred to the Robert Jones and Agnes Hunt Orthopaedic Hospital in Oswestry where he was a patient for many months. At times he longed to die but eventually returned home to Marton, as a paraplegic with some use of his upper limbs. He could play bridge with his friends, drive his car to work and was probably an excellent member of staff in the office where he worked, but his wife had left him and at home he was totally dependent on his mother for basic care. Other tragedies had occurred in the family – both his father and sister had died tragically, the latter I believe was murdered.

It was about 1975 when Noel wrote to the television programme *Crossroads*, recounting the difficulty his mother had in caring for him. He suggested, radically for the time, that carers should be supported in the work they undertook in looking after their disabled relatives. He pointed out their need for help, and the principle of 'Caring for the Carers' soon became widely accepted. It started in a small way. Money was raised to establish a local charity that later became the Cross Roads Care Charity and a local nurse was appointed to help Mrs Crane with Noel. Initially the main requirement was to help Noel get up in the morning, prepare him for going to work, and help him to bed at night. The nurse and the Cranes established a pattern of care which suited the household, and the scheme was gradually extended. Now under the aegis of the Cross Roads Care Charity a network of carers exists in the UK, with about 5,000 trained professionals available to support people of all ages who look after their disabled relatives.

Despite the tragedies that occurred within the Crane

family, Noel and his mother always seemed buoyant. It was one of those households in which I always felt enlivened when visiting. I remember speaking to Mrs Crane one day and asking her: "How do you manage to keep so cheerful and do so many good things in the village, with the problems you have had?" She replied: "I had a vision of my daughter, and she looked so radiant and beautiful, that I knew she was alright."

Village Helpers

Stretton-on-Dunsmore, Marton and Princethorpe were typical of the villages in the area. The people were remarkably friendly and helpful to one another and, as the new doctor, I benefitted from their kindness. The priests at Princethorpe College provided me with a house free of rent when I needed it, whilst the two cottages I had purchased at auction were being renovated and merged into a single dwelling for my family. The house was chosen by Valerie and has one of the best all-round views in Warwickshire. Drs Sylvia and Bill Cree, in the adjoining Wolston practice, were the best of neighbours. There was no competition between the practices and they helped in various ways, not least by covering the Stretton practice in my occasional absence. They even allowed me to raid their store of sweets (usually dolly mixtures) when I visited their surgery. In Marton, Jean Robson was full of good works though she had a family and large farmhouse to maintain, so too were the Reeves who farmed at Eathorpe.

The medical service provided by Bob Mac was a touch archaic when I moved in. Tablets and medicines were left in the porch of his house for collection by patients, or their friends, a system that may have worked well once but could not be continued indefinitely. The village shop and post office in Stretton was another repository for drugs, where people like Jean Robson collected them regularly for the villagers who had no transport. The packaging of medicines was becoming more standardised, with names and instructions being written in typescript and no longer by hand, and the amount of controlled drugs being prescribed was probably increasing even then. The system would have to change. Another uncertainty was the long-term availability of Kate's house as a centre for the practice surgery. Other premises would have to be found and I had no desire to build a new surgery or extend the practice – that was a task for a younger, more dynamic doctor. I was in no hurry to move but when St Mary's Hospice in Birmingham invited me to become its medical director, I accepted the job partly because of the encouragement Valerie gave me to do so, but also because of my concern, dating from my Llanidloes days, for appropriate care of the dying.

On my resigning as GP in Stretton-on-Dunsmore, Dr Menon was appointed to the practice. He had been brought up in southern India and had a flourishing practice in Bradford before deciding to move to a more rural part of England. The date for our joint move was agreed, but he placed more reliance on astrological assessments than I did and became quite alarmed when he realised that the change-over was scheduled for a date that astrologers regarded as most unpropitious. He phoned and asked me to change dates, which I agreed to do so as far as my new commitments would allow, and the handover was postponed for a few days. Unfortunately, Dr Menon had a heart attack within a few years of moving to Stretton-on-Dunsmore but, by then, he had bought a plot of land within the village where a new surgery could be constructed. His successor, Dr Michael Houghton, completed the project and the village now has a large purpose-built surgery with two partners, two GP-registrars, two nurses, three dispensers, three receptionists, a secretary and two practice managers. A phlebotomist, health visitor and midwife are also attached to the surgery. Obviously, the pattern of care is different from when one doctor managed the practice with the help of a single receptionist/dispenser, but people seem content with the present arrangements and the changes in practice and management were inevitable.

8

St Mary's Hospice
1980–90

SOMETIMES IN LLANIDLOES, I was asked to see people from Birmingham in the casualty department of the cottage hospital. Some had come to fish the River Severn, others to sail on Llyn Clywedog, or just to enjoy the beauty of the countryside. The medical problems they presented were usually minor, cuts requiring a few sutures or fishing hooks that were embedded in an eyelid and needed to be removed. That was over forty years ago and I remember little of these encounters, but I do recall a remark one visitor made to me. She said: "This is a lovely little hospital; I do wish we had one like it in Birmingham." My reply was: "There is no chance of you getting one like this." I was wrong, because Birmingham got St Mary's Hospice, which, though a specialised unit, provided the city with the close personal care that is a feature of cottage hospitals then and now.

I never expected to work in Birmingham but in a circuitous way I became medical director of St Mary's Hospice and was regarded, at least initially, as the expert on palliative care for the city. It was not such an unusual appointment for a general practitioner to be given then as, apart from St Christopher's Hospice, there were no training posts for palliative care physicians in those days, and few doctors had even a basic knowledge of the principles governing terminal care. Unusually for a GP, I had cared for patients within bedded units for most of my working life, and as mentioned earlier, my research interests had included bereavement and the care of the dying. 'The Distress of Dying', written in Llanidloes, was one of the first attempts to record the experiences of the terminally ill, and to do so in a way that could be charted by nurses.[23] The method never became widely used but, before undertaking the study, I had spent a week with Cicely Saunders soon after she opened St Christopher's Hospice in 1967, and learnt something of the methods she was advocating in this the first modern hospice. It was a brief introduction but more than most doctors enjoyed. At that time Cicely was using oral diamorphine as the analgesic of choice for minimising terminal pain, a practice I followed until oral morphine was shown to be equally effective. One reason for my going to Birmingham was that the trustees had difficulty in finding a suitable applicant for the job and seemed keen to have me. This was partly because St Mary's wished to become recognised as the main centre for teaching palliative care in Birmingham, and the trustees thought that I would be an effective teacher. Experience as a GP was important too, as it enabled the family practitioner committee to appoint me as a general practitioner within the hospice. This had important financial implications because it enabled patients admitted to St Mary's (registered as a nursing home) to be registered as temporary residents under my care as a GP, and for the drugs they needed to be provided by the NHS. However, the most important reason for my going to Birmingham was that Valerie thought that I should do so.

St Mary's Hospice

St Mary's Hospice was opened in March 1979 with 20 beds. It had no teaching centre and no day centre; these were established later during my time at the hospice. The first patient to be admitted was received by Sister Mary, a nun (Sister of Charity) and trained nurse, who instinctively knelt as the patient entered the hospice, symbolising the warmth and care that awaited all patients who came there. It was opened during the second phase of the developing hospice movement, being the first independent hospice in the Midlands and only the seventh nationwide. The idea for its establishment was discussed initially by Monica Pearce (the retired matron of Birmingham General Hospital) and Paddy Mitchell (a Catholic priest) as they sheltered from the rain in the porch of St Chad's Roman Catholic Cathedral in Birmingham. Ms Pearce, mentioned her wish to establish a hospice for the terminally ill in Birmingham, and Fr Mitchell replied "let's get on with it". Together they formed a committee and started to raise money for their new hospice, with Fr Mitchell acting as chairman of the inaugural committee and Ms Pearce being the driving force behind the project. Their efforts were successful – the money flowed in and the Catholic archbishop allocated a house, which had formerly been a mother and babies unit, to provide a centre for the hospice. A local architect was commissioned to redesign the building, which he did not only tastefully but with a layout well suited for the care of the patients, and St Mary's Hospice was established in Selly Park, Birmingham.

Teething Problems

Not surprisingly, there were teething troubles. Financing the project was, and has always been, a problem, but the money continued to be found and the scope of the work expanded. The charismatic Ms Pearce attracted some of the best nurses in Birmingham to St Mary's, but of these only the senior sister had worked in a hospice before and she left within a year. With the initial intake containing many senior nurses, staff expectations were high, in some instances too high, and some nurses even accepted a reduction in salary to work at St Mary's, which was commendable but not always wise. This was my own position when I joined, though its effect on the family finances was never discussed with the management. Fr Mitchell's sudden decision to leave St Mary's was another blow, especially for me as we had got on particularly well together. One day, quite unexpectedly, he asked for a quiet word and said, "Dewi, I am leaving to get married and will not be here tomorrow. Will you let the staff know?" Sadly from that moment Paddy Mitchell ceased to be associated with St Mary's, and his early, influential role was never mentioned again. He joined the Anglican Church and became a vicar in south-east England.

Medical Care

When I arrived at the hospice, a young GP, John Wozniak, and two retired doctors provided the medical care in the wards, each being in charge on successive days. One of the retired doctors was a former GP, the other a consultant obstetrician. All three were essential for the early establishment of the hospice, and John Wozniak remained a pivotal figure for almost thirty years. Moreover, they received no remuneration whilst I was there. They met once a week with the social worker and senior nurses, but had no other regular contact with each other. Each prescribed as they considered best and there was a tendency for the drugs prescribed one day to be cancelled or increased the next day, which may have influenced the level of opiates prescribed as mentioned in my paper 'The opioid needs of terminal care patients'.[24] The situation improved considerably when Simon Dover was appointed medical registrar and established a consistent pattern of prescribing on the wards. He wrote the first paper on the use of the syringe driver in the domiciliary care of the terminally ill to be published in the *British Medical Journal* and, with Dr Low-Beer and myself, published another paper entitled 'Terminal cancer patients referred for hospice care who did not have cancer and were not terminally ill'.[25] In it we described how four patients, who had been referred to the hospice with terminal cancer, happily were found not to have the disease. There was nothing deliberate about the errors, but it seems unlikely that such mistakes occur in the catchment area of only one hospice – they must occur elsewhere also, but at that stage had not been reported.

As the medical director at St Mary's I worked on the wards, and covered nights and weekends, but most of the time was spent on administration, teaching and with the home care team. In addition to signing the death and cremation certificates, and writing to doctors, I undertook a range of administrative duties, attending the many education, planning and general purpose committees that were essential during that early phase of the hospice's growth, when plans were discussed to build a new day centre and a teaching block. A bereavement service and a basic lecture programme had been established before I joined the hospice, but the demand for training in palliative care was great and I was the only trainer in the unit until Sr Mary was eventually given the role of nurse tutor. Arrangements were already in place for trainee-GPs to visit the hospice and I had the task of teaching them. They attended fortnightly in groups of about 30 doctors and seemed to find the experience useful and inspiring. Final-year students from the university's department of general practice visited the hospice each week, usually in pairs, and I would take them on domiciliary visits with a Macmillan nurse, which was a good way to introduce them to the practicalities as well as emotional aspects of terminal care. As part of their clinical programme, I was also asked to provide medical students with a formal lecture at the end of their gynaecological course, and to supervise their dissertations on terminal care for the department of social medicine. In addition I taught various aspects of palliative medical and nursing care more widely, and eventually there was not a hospital in Birmingham and its neighbouring towns where I did not speak to multidisciplinary audiences. It was quite demanding, especially as we continued to live in rural Warwickshire about 30 miles from the hospice. One pleasing outcome was my being appointed an honorary senior clinical lecturer by the University of Birmingham in recognition of the teaching I provided for the medical faculty.

Home Care Team (HCT)

As a general practitioner, I had a special interest in the care of the terminally ill at home. This was provided at St Mary's by the hospice's home care team, which was funded by Macmillan Care and was the first HCT to be established in the Midlands. Home care teams do not provide hands-on nursing care, which remains the role of district nurses, but they have a special expertise in symptom management and in supporting terminally ill patients and their families. The team leader was Joan Barlow, a health visitor and the first Macmillan nurse to be appointed in the region. She soon attracted Pat Serafinas (a senior nurse) and Joanna (a social worker from New Zealand) into her team. All were in post when I arrived. It was a happy group and particularly welcoming, as they were eager to involve me in their work. They had an office at the top of the building which was fine, but initially they felt isolated, as they had little medical support and were not allowed any real contact with their patients once they were admitted to the wards. We arranged to meet each morning to discuss their patients, and I would see those for whom they had specific concerns. One of them always accompanied me during a home visit and they never allowed me to drive the car. Medical students often joined us on these visits, obtaining a real insight into the care of patients at home and the support needed by their families.

They also encountered a range of cultures and ethnic groups, as our Macmillan nurses had access to people of various religious and cultural backgrounds. With them I gained entry into the homes of people of most major religious faiths, and some even invited us to attend their mourning ceremonies when those in our care had passed away. "When is Dr Rees coming to see us?" one Hindu family asked Joanna. So we went together and attended the ritual ceremony for the dead mother. The family was most welcoming and it was good to see her young children moving happily around the house whilst her soul was being blessed and helped into the next phase of her life. In those early days the home care team would regularly attend their patient's funerals, and if the deceased had no known living relatives we were sometimes the only mourners present. One funeral director told us after such an occasion: "I much rather have you at the funeral than some family members, because I know you want to be here."

Following the death of a Sikh youth from cancer, the family invited us to the *akhand path*, a complete public reading of the *Guru Granth Sahib*, the Sikh sacred scriptures, written in the ancient *Gurmukhi* script. This reading lasts for 10–13 days and we were honoured by the invitation and managed to attend part of a session. For the ceremony, a room in the house had been converted into a *gurdwara*, a Sikh temple. The room was cleared of all furniture and hangings, and replaced by a *maji*, a covered dais surmounted by a canopy, a *palki*. Cushions were placed on the dais, the *Guru Granth Sahib* were set on the cushions, and portraits of the Sikh gurus (religious leaders) were placed on the walls. This converted the room into a temple and a succession of readers, men and women, then read the holy scriptures from beginning to end. People entering the room did so shoeless with their heads covered by a turban, veil or clean cloth. We were allowed to place a clean handkerchief on our heads. On entering we knelt before the *Guru Granth Sahib*, and placed money at the base of the dais as a contribution to the communal food and the poor. Then we sat on the floor to hear the reading. The senior elder honoured us by inviting me to sit next to him and then providing a detailed explanation of the ceremony, and giving me a copy of the Sikh prayers that he had translated into English. It was both a remarkable and a moving experience.

Naturally I remember other incidents and some of the homes I visited. There was a young woman who asked me to visit her at home, where she lived alone, as she wanted to arrange her own admission to the hospice, not immediately, but when she could no longer cope by herself. She had incurable disseminated cancer, and was prepared to accept the treatment the doctors planned for her whilst knowing that it would not affect the course of the disease. As I left the house she offered me a Mars chocolate bar, which I accepted, and that was the pattern she established with everyone. Whoever visited her at home or in the hospice was offered a small gift before they left. It might be just a grape or two, but the offer was always made. In the hospice, she became a great favourite with the nurses and one of her last requests was to be taken to a swimming pool so she could swim just once more. She was not in the pool long but her wish was attained. That complied with hospice policy, for every effort was made for patients' wishes to be fulfilled. A middle-aged lady wanted to go to the Chelsea Flower Show. The notice given was short but Joanna, the social worker, managed to get the tickets and funding for the trip, and accompanied her to the show. It was a great success, as was the visit to Dudley Zoo that the nurses arranged for a man with motor neurone disease; he wanted to see an elephant before he died. Fortunately, hospices are themselves the benefactors of many peoples' goodwill, as the following case indicates. Our Macmillan nurses had helped a young Jewish doctor to care for his wife at home, and when she died, he arranged a concert in memory of his wife. The concert was well attended and with the other funds he raised, the young widower presented the hospice with a cheque for £20,000.

Another memory that is fixed firmly in my mind, was being asked to see a fifteen-year-old girl with an osteosarcoma of the thigh. The tumour was so large that it pinned her to the mattress on the floor where she lay. She was the only child of divorced parents and was looked after by her father in a terraced house. Three friends were waiting to see her when the nurse and I arrived but we were given precedence and allowed to see the girl first. During our conversation I asked her about the friends and their thoughts about her future. She smiled and said, "You are asking about the afterlife. I tell them, I shall come back and haunt them." On another occasion I received a telephone call from a lady who asked if Professor Wales could visit the hospice. I said "Yes, of course," and then because her voice was not clear added, "Who is speaking please?" She said, "I am a Lady in Waiting to the Princess of Wales, and she would like to visit the hospice". When Princess Diana arrived a few weeks later, the visit was a delight for all at St Mary's and the many spectators who gathered outside to see her. Not long afterwards, I received an invitation to a garden party at Buckingham Palace, which Valerie and I both enjoyed immensely.

St Mary's Hospice has expanded greatly in the past 30 years. It now has conference facilities in addition to an enlarged teaching unit, and most of the original building has been restructured and renovated. Many more nurses are employed on the home care team and the pattern of care within the hospice has changed also, with more patients being admitted for short-term care and appraisal, before returning home. This is the pattern everywhere; the hospice movement is now a worldwide movement, with palliative care facilities being available in every continent, and possibly most countries. At the same time, palliative medicine has developed with enormous speed as a separate speciality, and opportunities to train for consultant posts in palliative nursing, medicine, and social work are increasing and becoming more readily available.

9

Retirement 1990–2012

I DID NOT expect to retire when I was sixty. I thought that I would work many years more, but I was exhausted after ten years at the hospice. Part of the trouble was residing outside Birmingham, as the distance travelling to work was excessive but that was my choice. Also, as a GP, I was accustomed to a more varied pattern of work than in terminal care, and to be constantly involved with the dying is sustainable only if one has sensible holidays and working arrangements, which I failed to arrange for myself. Not surprisingly, something had to give and the inevitable heart attack struck me soon after I retired. My survival and long-term recovery was due to the skill and kindness of Dr Martin Been and the cardiac team at Coventry's Walsgrave Hospital. Recovery was slow but twenty years was added to a life which, in 2006, was saddened by the death of Valerie, my wife for 54 years. Since retiring I have published three books, and am writing this fourth (and perhaps final) book to record the many changes I have seen in my life as a medical practitioner. So how does present practice compare with the past? The answer depends of course on one's perspective, and I am now more likely to receive rather than to give medical care, but I would say less well than is often portrayed by the leaders of our speciality. There have been big improvements in salary and conditions of service for GPs, but much has also been lost. At times my own life was too busy, but it was varied and interesting, and sometimes I received a letter from other doctors expressing a wish to have the lifestyle we enjoyed in Llanidloes.

The Computer Era

One notable difference with general practice today is that the close links with individuals and communities appear to be breaking down. This is inevitable, partly because the structure of society is changing, but also because the nature of general practice has also changed. I discussed it recently with my daughter Anna, who lives in south Wales. She seems very happy with the care her family receives from their general practitioners but, whilst the practice has six doctors, mainly women, only three work full-time, i.e. for a five day week. Perhaps more significantly, the 24-hour 7-day week has been replaced by sensible office hours, and doctors generally work from 8.30 a.m. in the morning to 4 or 6 p.m. at night, from Monday to Friday only, with out-of-hours cover provided by an agency. Practitioners no longer live in a house attached to the surgery, as separate purpose-built surgeries have become the norm, and the need to live within the practice area is not considered imperative. Patients are still seen by a practice doctor immediately if necessary, but the waiting time to see a doctor of one's choice is often surprisingly long, as much as three to five weeks. On the plus side, the system encourages doctors to develop special interests, so one can choose to be seen by the skin expert or the doctor with a special interest in arthritis or gynaecological problems. This is good, but it does reduce the likelihood of other doctors dealing with those problems, and honing their own skills and becoming general practitioners in the wider sense of the term.

In retrospect, the hours we spent on call were undoubtedly onerous, and partly contributed to my withdrawing from general practice both on leaving Llanidloes and again in Warwickshire, so the more measured working week must be helpful both for the doctor's own welfare and for attracting and retaining the next generation to family medicine. Yet I still feel regretful that the links between doctors and their patients seem weaker than they once were, and hope that future changes in the management of general practice will strengthen this important relationship. It should of course be noted that practices are not all run in the same way. My daughter Anna speaks of a useful arrangement that her GPs have with the local pharmacist. After each morning clinic, a member of the pharmacy collects the prescriptions from the surgery, so that prescribed medicines become available as soon as possible. That seems an excellent arrangement, more helpful than the present system in some dispensing practices where patients are required to wait 48 hours before they can collect their prescriptions. Such helpful management initiatives can make a big difference to patients' experiences.

In the old days prescriptions, and a patient's notes, were written by hand whereas now it is done on a computer. The benefits of the new system are many but I find the computer a distracting influence when I consult my GP, or the nurse who more frequently sees me. Anna's GP records her notes when the consultation is over, but that is not my experience now, or in the recent past when I was allowed to sit alongside other GPs as they were seeing their patients. The computer provides instant access to the patient's medical history, but I don't see how the doctor's attention can be fully devoted to the patient when so much information has to be extracted and recorded electronically. Computers have numerous benefits and I generally enjoy using them – including writing this book on one – but the keyboard and screen do require attention in a way that written notes did not demand of the practitioner. It cannot be easily ignored. I first learnt this at the age of 75 when I was allowed to return to general practice for a while, and obtained an insider's view of present practice. It was an eye-opener in many ways, and I am grateful to the friends who accepted me into their surgery, despite my being new to electronic note taking.

Academia and Change

When I qualified in 1956, the status of general practice was very low, and most ambitious doctors aimed to become hospital consultants. Lord Moran, then president of the Royal College of Physicians (and Winston Churchill's personal physician during the war) expressed the general view in these succinct words, "They have", he said, "fallen off the ladder". Since then the status of general practice has improved considerably, and the credit for this belongs mainly to the Royal College of General Practitioners. The British Medical Association has also done much to improve the remuneration and terms of service of doctors, but it is the Royal College of General Practitioners that sought to increase the academic status of family doctors. Now there are many academic departments of general practice in the UK, when previously there were none, and great importance is given to the training, and continued development of GPs. This has been associated with a great improvement in the premises from which general practitioners work.

When I joined Dr Myers' practice in 1957, he was a typical urban GP working with limited facilities in his own home. He had no ancillary help, not even a receptionist. By 1978, when I was appointed as sole practitioner at Stretton-on-Dunsmore in Warwickshire, conditions had improved generally and I worked in a pleasant purpose-built surgery with a dispenser-receptionist. Since then, further changes have been made within the practice. A new surgery has been built and a very fine building it is, with various consulting rooms, a clinical area for the nurse, a dispensary, a large waiting area, and a room upstairs where the staff can meet. Fifteen people work there now of which four are doctors; most are ancillary staff and they represent a big numerical increase from when Dr McElwain managed the practice. Most of the people employed in the surgery are women, which again reflects the changing pattern of general practice nationwide. Another helpful change was brought to my attention by a friend who told me that her GP had phoned her that morning on discovering in the practice records that she had fallen twice and broken two bones (humerus and radius) in recent years. The need to maintain bone density was discussed and Julie agreed to take the suggested medication, namely supplementary calcium and bisphosphonates. They agreed that there was no need for the two to meet and that Julie would collect the tablets from the surgery the next day. This is an efficient and effective way of dealing with a potential problem, and an aspect of preventive medicine that is increasingly practised and encouraged by the Government and the Royal College of General Practitioners.

The teaching of general practice as a separate speciality is a late development in the history of medical education. The College of General Practitioners was founded in 1952, receiving its royal charter in 1972 more than 450 years after the physicians received their royal charter. Academic departments of general practice began to emerge after World War II, first in Edinburgh and then in Sheffield; most significantly, these centres were closely associated with departments of public health and social medicine, the branches of medicine that are particularly interested in the way in which social and economic conditions can affect health and disease. Dr Richard Scott, a member of the academic department of public health and social medicine in Edinburgh, began the trend. On 12 July 1948 he established a small teaching and research unit that by 1951 provided 30 medical students with a three-month course on family medicine in Edinburgh. In 1963 he was appointed the first professor of general practice in the world. This was followed by similar appointments elsewhere, including the appointment at St Thomas's Hospital Medical School of the first senior lecturer in general practice in London, and a similar post at the Welsh National School of Medicine in Cardiff. As at Edinburgh, these posts were placed initially within academic departments of social medicine. I was interviewed for both the London and Cardiff posts but not appointed. In 1973, I was offered, quite unexpectedly, a senior lecturer's post at Guy's Hospital but, despite feeling greatly honoured at the approach, decided not to take it. Before then, Professor Scott had phoned me about a post in his department, but Edinburgh seemed very far away, and so different from mid Wales.

Now there are many departments of general practice worldwide, and I wonder what type of doctors they seek to produce. Do the young people who become general practitioners in the UK have the same expectations and experience as those who graduate elsewhere – in Australia, China, Canada, India or the USA? These are questions I cannot resolve, but no UK graduate would expect, or be able, to do the work Dr Graham Davies undertook for the mining families of Tredegar in the 1920s, and later in rural mid Wales, nor does society expect it of them. So much has changed. The ethos of social medicine has become part of general practice and with it some loss of the personal relationship between doctor and patient that is an essential feature of general practice. The work done is good and patients are content, but so much is undertaken by other agencies (by paramedics, practice nurses, healthcare assistants, etc.) that it can no longer be truly called general practice in the broad sense of that term. It is also much more systematic than it used to be, for instance monitoring patients' health electronically and informing them when they should be seen. Last autumn I was called for a routine health check, and within a few days went to the surgery four times before an assessment of my medication by a doctor was considered necessary. Then, following a telephone consultation, amlodipine was added to my regime. It was effective and I suppose all that was needed, yet this small change seemed to require so much time and effort by the patient, as well as the staff.

Valerie's Death

I do get upset when I think of my wife's death. One morning she complained of a painful knee, which I mistakenly considered to be a haemarthrosis (bleeding into the joint) as she was taking aspirin, following a recent heart attack. The joint became more painful in the evening, so we sent for a paramedic, as no doctor was available to visit her, and she was taken to the largest A & E unit in the area, where she was not seen for some hours. I expected the knee to be aspirated and her pain eased, but instead was told the knee could not be treated in that hospital and she was to be transferred to another unit. After much delay she was placed on antibiotics and sent to the second hospital, where she was not seen by a doctor until late afternoon, when an orthopaedic registrar aspirated the knee and removed a small amount of mucky fluid. Then he phoned his consultant and told us that Valerie was to be transferred to a third hospital that night as the knee needed to be 'washed out' under general anaesthesia. I saw no reason for this but, as we were told that Valerie would be the first on the operating list in the morning, I did not demur. Valerie accepted all these decisions without complaint, but it was late afternoon before she was taken to the theatre where the knee was declared dry. Throughout this period of hospitalisation, she was confined to bed by an intravenous drip and a urethral catheter and was given little to eat or drink except sandwiches. Moreover, I was not allowed to visit her in the third hospital until she had been to theatre. The next day she was moved to the intensive care unit where she died on the Saturday afternoon, having been admitted to the first hospital on Monday evening. I am sure she would not have died if she had seen my old partner Graham Davies. He would have taken her to the cottage hospital, aspirated the knee, placed her on antibiotics and sent her back home to the family. If she had been given that basic treatment when the paramedics had taken her into the first hospital, she would have recovered quickly and soon been home. Instead she was moved twice and died in the intensive care unit of a dilapidated hospital that was to be closed within a few weeks. I had never been inside an intensive care unit before, it was so different from the hospice care that I had practised and taught. The nurses were efficient and kind, but we were kept at a distance and the drips, catheters and respirator that enmeshed Valerie stopped me getting close to her and holding her. Nor could I speak to her, and say the things that needed to be said, as I could not get sufficiently close to express the private thoughts that I wished to share.

Education

I became a Fellow of the Royal College of General Practitioners (FRCGP) in 1972, having been an associate and member before that date, I joined the college's south Wales faculty board in 1962, and became a regular attendee at its meetings which were held in Cardiff on a Sunday. One of the first things we had to decide was which of the two college priorities, either education or research, each member intended to pursue individually. Most faculty board members chose education, only a few chose research. I was in the latter group and joined the research committee. Nothing memorable was discussed at these meetings, but they did provide an opportunity to spend time with like-minded people. Nor did we discuss those other important concerns of general practitioners – their remuneration and terms of service – as the British Medical Association had considerable experience in negotiating those matters. Anyway, the financial aspects of medical practice has never really concerned me, and I would not want to be involved in the management of NHS funding which the Government plans to hand over to general practitioners in England at the next reorganisation of the NHS. I am sure there are GPs who will welcome the new opportunity this provides, but it will require a significant change in attitude to general practice that would not be congenial to me.

In 2004–5 I attended the regular (fortnightly) training courses for GP-registrars in my area, but whilst the sessions were popular with the registrars and had a useful social aspect, I was not greatly impressed by the instruction given. I found the content remarkably limited, and the teaching style mainly auditory. Briefly, the teaching seemed to be centred on just three aspects of general practice, viz. avoiding litigation, making money and passing the MRCGP examination. The nature of general practice outside the UK was never discussed. This was surprising as students attending the course included doctors from Africa, India and the Ukraine, but no attempt was made to include their much wider experience, and different background, into the content of the course.

I am told people learn in three different ways: visual, auditory and kinaesthetic (learning by doing). Whilst most people use all three methods to some degree, each individual has a preferred style of learning, with kinaesthetic learners being the commonest (about 37 per cent of the population), followed by auditory learners (34 per cent) and visual learners (29 per cent). The style of teaching on the training course was preponderantly auditory, with few visual presentations, and even less kinaesthetic teaching. I recall only two practical sessions: one was on cardiopulmonary resuscitation and the other on suturing wounds. I was surprised that doctors who had been qualified for at least a year needed to practise such a basic skill as suturing. What, I wondered, had they been taught during their years of training as medical students and hospital doctors? At least the need for further training is recognised now and courses of instruction are available. It was not so when I entered general practice in 1957. Then a training programme was only beginning to emerge and, when my trainer became ill a few weeks after I joined his practice (during which time I had learnt about the administrative aspects of general practice), I was left to manage by myself, which I did not find too difficult. On completing my training year, there were no other programmes in place for further training and I had to gain experience by seeking posts I thought might be helpful and which would provide a useful income for my family. Eventually I spent five years learning my job before I became a principal in general practice. Then I was fortunate to join a group practice with probably the best GP of his generation in the country.

Other Doctor's Views

The practice of family medicine has changed enormously in my lifetime. Society and the participating doctors seem pleased with the changes but there are a few dissenting voices, and because they deserve a platform I include two of their comments here. I start with a letter from a friend who I had not seen for many years. He is a retired GP who wrote:

> I joined the College of General Practitioners in about 1960. I stuck with the college and its apotheosis into the Royal College of General Practitioners but when they introduced the obligatory exam, I sent in my resignation as I don't believe Pickles would have approved. It was, I believe, meant to be a beacon in the darkness of general practice which attracted by example and precept, not another wretched exam with the eventual progress to lecturers and professors, etc.

When the MRCGP became a necessary postgraduate qualification for general practitioners, like my friend I felt sorry for the doctors who would have to sit the exam and was glad that I did not have to surmount that obstacle. Nor was William Pickles required to take the examination. Pickles was a country doctor in North Yorkshire who published an account, in 1930, of an epidemic of catarrhal jaundice in Wensleydale that affected 250 people. He was able to trace the entire epidemic to one child and show that the incubation period lasted 26 to 35 days.[26] He undertook other epidemiological studies, including one on Bornholm disease (epidemic myalgia), and in 1939 published a book *Epidemiology of General Practice*, which became a medical classic. He continued working as a country doctor until 1964 and became the first president of the Royal College of General Practitioners.

Another friend, who I had known for many years, was furious when he told me of his experience with his GP. I had never seen him so angry before. He had gone to the surgery to discuss a clinical problem with his doctor. No one was in the waiting room or at the reception desk, and there were only two cars outside. He heard his doctor talking in the background, then he came to the reception area. He told him of his problem but the GP was totally dismissive, saying that he was too busy to speak to him, and in any case he could not be referred for the treatment he required. Poor man, he was in his late-seventies and was only seeking basic help. I know him as a caring doctor who would never have turned any patient away. Now he says, "I am glad I am no longer a GP, they are no longer interested in their patients". No doubt, as in any profession, some doctors have always been more sympathetic than others, and even the best of doctors will have occasional off days. But courtesy is a constant requirement, and listening to patients remains crucial for prompt and accurate diagnosis of illness at any time.

Research in Perspective

When I became a general practitioner in 1957, the status of the speciality was low in comparison with other branches of medicine. Now the situation is different but some of the old attitude remains. This was made apparent by an article on GP research published in 2009,[27] forty-five years after my first paper appeared in the *British Medical Journal*. I have always been interested in medical research and it was a great thrill for me to have two papers published in an international journal in 1965, and I considered it an achievement for general practice as well as myself. So I was disappointed to read in the *British Journal of General Practice* that the early research, which a few of us undertook, is best described as being merely "occupational therapy for doctors". The authors also say that "the days of the gentlemen amateur working to produce research in a general practice cottage industry are now over" and that the "impact of single practitioner research studies are limited (and) rarely results in a major contribution to the sum of our clinical knowledge". I do hope not. I wonder what William Pickles would have said and if my peer-reviewed papers published in those early years are as useless as the writers suggest. Moreover, it is interesting to note that the basic approach of many of today's studies is not that used by William Pickles; there is relatively little face-to-face contact with the patients, but a greater reliance on the mass survey and multidisciplinary approach of social medicine. This large scale research is fine in its own sphere and it is important for confirming population-level trends and medical benefits, but I question whether it can truly be described as general practice research which, as Murdoch discussed in his article in the BJGP,[28] provides opportunities for initiating questions as well as involving more detailed, qualitative research.

Similarly in their robust response to the 2009 BJGP article, members of the Honiton Group Practice, defending the role of the practice-based primary care research, cited their strong publication record in fields ranging from teenage sexual health to anticoagulant monitoring,[29] and such work is most welcome. Yet, if we examine the papers on general practice published today, we find that few researchers are personally involved with the populations they study. For instance, a 2010 edition of the *British Journal of General Practice* contains seven original articles, written by 32 researchers and involving 16,412 patients, so it is unlikely that any researcher spoke to many patients.[30] These papers are mostly epidemiological studies involving research scientists attached to specialist units in the UK (for instance the General Practice Research Database of the Medicines and Healthcare Products Regulatory Agency, the Health Protection Agency Centre for Infections, and the Research Department of Infections and Population Health, University College London) and other parts of Europe, such as the Collaborating Centre for International Drug Monitoring in Sweden. In only one of the papers was a researcher likely to have had any direct involvement with the patients studied. This was a paper on angina written by a nurse, two-primary care doctors and a non-medical Ph.D. Whilst it is important to include large numbers of patients in some studies to ensure that the results hold for the population as a whole, they should not replace the more detailed studies involving individual patients that general practice is so well positioned to undertake.

A comparison made by Professor Murdoch of the number of research studies published over six-month periods in 1968 and 2008 indicated that the proportion of GP authors had declined substantially. I surveyed papers recently published in the BJGP over a slightly longer period (91 articles which appeared in the journal in 2010) and similarly found that only nine were by GPs, or appeared to include GPs as co-authors; in contrast, over 70 per cent were led by researchers at universities. What perhaps is more surprising is the focus of the research, with 42 of the papers being on GP performance, compared with 40 focusing on the patients, three papers on both GPs and their patients and six on financial and management matters.[31] It is possible that, if GPs are seconded to universities, the inclusion of a university address may under represent GPs' involvement in initiating and taking forward research during literature reviews. I hope that this is the case, but meanwhile remain concerned that

GPs' knowledge of their patients and analytical abilities are underestimated and underused.

I would like to see the Royal College of General Practitioners do more to encourage individual research by GPs in their own practices. This is the type of research that William Pickles undertook and we learnt a great deal from him. I worked as a lone researcher in Llanidloes, and later as a member of the Whitehall 2 Study in London, and consider that the former was much more interesting than the latter. On reflection, I think it also had the advantage of being zero additional cost to the Government and the taxpayer. Field work, analyses and writing were done in my own time and I paid all the publication costs myself. I am perhaps not best placed to assess whether the effort was worthwhile but would like to think that this independent research did serve to improve medical knowledge and provide some benefit to practitioners and patients. A full list of my publications is given as an Appendix to this book, but the most useful period was probably between 1965–72, when I published nine papers (including six in the *British Medical Journal*) when I was at Llanidloes. Two of the papers were written with the help of Sylvia Lutkins (a statistician at UCW Aberystwyth) and are still cited in books and scientific papers. Of these, the 'Mortality of Bereavement' was mentioned in 2005 by Joan Didion (a novelist) in *The Year of Magical Thinking*,[32] whilst the 'Hallucinations of Widowhood' is quoted in his writings of 2003 and 2011 by Gerald O'Collins[33] and in 2008 by Christine Valentine, a teacher at the Centre for Death and Society at Bath University.[34] An earlier paper, 'Agricultural Tractor Accidents', which the *British Medical Journal* published in 1965, is never cited, but possibly because it received so much media coverage that it may have influenced Parliament to pass a Bill in 1967 requiring all new agricultural tractors to be fitted with a safety cab. Since then the number of deaths in the UK from overturning tractors has fallen considerably. The much larger Whitehall 2 study has had no direct effect on mortality, but it has provided a better understanding of the important relationship that exists between hierarchical status and personal health among public employees. So it seems to me that both approaches to research are of value to society and should be encouraged, but let us not forget the importance of individual research in general practice.

Whilst personal research is a desirable aim, few GPs attempt it. That is understandable as it is essentially a minority interest and can be socially isolating. In Llanidloes I worked in a group practice, but was fortunate that my surgery was located in my own house, and I had a great deal of independence as a researcher which suited me well. I was not required to consult with anyone in advance about the work, or to obtain permission to take it forward, so had the space to let ideas develop. These days, when life seems more structured, there are more formalities to observe, with committees required to approve the work and senior people to be consulted. Consultation with experts in the field is essential for developing new concepts and for ensuring that the research is both sound and novel, but I am told it can be a bit daunting if not handled sympathetically. This is an area where senior doctors will be keen to help young GPs, bearing in mind that people with innovative ideas can be easily flattened emotionally, and their desire to pursue a research project lost.

I have no experience of supporting people in developing their research but anticipate that in this financially competitive field people would wish for advice on the best fundraising agencies to approach and how to submit grant applications effectively. The Royal College of General Practioners has recently been active in establishing funding and support for GP researchers, for instance through the development in 1994 of RCGP Research General Practices with finance to put in place some research infrastructure and research work within the practice.[35] By the autumn of 1995, fourteen research general practices had been funded in this way and, although somewhat atypical (for instance, they were largely non-urban), were considered exceptionally well placed for developing research into general practice.[36] More recently, although Research General Practices are still active and attract some research funding, this is usually associated with larger studies, and is more likely to involve helping researchers' access patients. It is notable that, although the grants awarded by the National Institute for Health Research (NIHR) are open to "all NHS providers (including research general practices) in England", it also requires that this be "in collaboration with an appropriate academic partner or partners". I therefore hope that the Royal College will do yet more to encourage individual research by GPs particularly in their own practices, and look beyond the large-scale, multidisciplinary research that has become the norm. I know there are practitioners who would welcome this development.

A Final Assessment

Sixty years have passed since I started my medical career as a student at St Thomas's Hospital on the South Bank of the river Thames. In those post World War II days, London was a bleaker but safer place than now. Rationing was still in force, and the autumn smog was sometimes so thick it was difficult to see the person walking immediately in front of you. But the streets were safe and, after leaving Valerie near her hostel by Baker Street, I would walk across the city to my lodgings in Streatham without any fear of being attacked or hindered. It was an exciting time medically. People with tuberculosis were being cured with streptomycin and INAH, and so many new drugs and techniques had become available that I remember thinking as a GP in Eltham that, despite my inexperience, I had resources that enabled me to be a more effective doctor than even the best consultants who had practised in London in the 1930s. The following year, accompanied by my wife and young child, I was in Labrador where the conditions and expectations were totally different. The air was clean and unpolluted, the vistas extensive, and instead of visiting patients by car I did so by airplane, boat, snowmobile and dog-sleigh. There I had to accept responsibilities that no new doctor in the UK would have to undertake, but it was one reason I went there, and I relished and benefited from the experience. Then, when we returned home, I was fortunate to be given a job as a junior doctor in one of the best psychiatric units in the country. Suddenly the pattern changed. My practice was no longer large stretches of Labrador where I had an independent role, but was restricted to a hospital building and its outlying clinics, where I worked alongside more senior doctors.

I could have remained in psychiatry but my intention had always been to be a GP, so after a year in psychiatry I moved to mid Wales, to Llanidloes where I spent the most intense and productive 13 years of my professional life. It grieved me to leave the practice but I knew I should do so, and my wife and family supported my decision. Then I returned to London and became a civil servant, which offered me an insight into an entirely different form of medicine, and medical research. It was great but not my milieu, then I found my feet again as a GP in Warwickshire, a beautiful county but not quite the same as mid Wales.

Finally I became a hospice doctor and helped to further the practice and teaching of palliative medicine among the doctors, nurses and medical students of Birmingham, and in its neighbourhoods. Mine has been a wonderfully varied life. There have been moments of great tension, joy and sadness. I hope that I have been helpful and kind to other people, to my family and patients, and anyone else I may have affected by my life, teachings and writings. Naturally, I have not been idle since retiring. For many years I was a voluntary guide at Coventry Cathedral, a role I greatly enjoyed, and for some years conducted the fortnightly healing services at the cathedral. I was never sure of their effectiveness but found them helpful to myself and was surprised by the number of people who told me, in private, that they too were helped by these services. Most often they said that attending the services helped them to sleep at night, not just on the night of the service itself but for the full fortnight between meetings. Another voluntary task came my way from a chance meeting with a prison chaplain. She asked me to help at a young offenders institute, which I did. My role was mainly that of a bereavement counsellor, and I was amazed at the large number of young men I was asked to see, who had suffered serious bereavements in their early life. Now I am properly retired. I am a widower, and have Charcot-Marie-Tooth disease, a hereditary problem which affects the nerve pathways and makes walking more difficult. But I have good friends and splendid children, and am still capable of managing my life alone. I am indeed a fortunate man.

APPENDIX

Other Publications by Dewi Rees

Papers not mentioned in the text

'Psychotropic drugs and the motorist', *The Practitioner*, 196 (1966), p.704.

'Parental depression before and after childbirth', *Journal of the Royal College of General Practitioners*, 21 (1971), p.26. (with Lutkins)

'Pulmonary embolus', *British Medical Journal*, 2 (1972), p.102. (with Jenkins)

'Bereavement and illness', *Journal of Thanatology*, 2 (1972), p.814.

'The Distress of Dying', *American Heart Journal*, 86 (1973), p.141.

'Role of the hospice in the care of the dying', *British Medical Journal*, 285 (1982), p.1,768.

'Making contact with the recently bereaved', *The Practitioner*, 228 (1984), p.309.

'Immigrants and the hospice', *Health Trends*, 18 (1986) p.89.

'The Mortality associated with respite care in a hospice', *Palliative Medicine*, 1 (1987), p.163.

'Terminal care in hospital, hospice and general practice. A comparison between 1981 and 1986', *Journal of the Royal College of General Practitioners*, 37 (1988), p.501.

'The Opioid needs of terminal care patients: variations with age and primary site', *Clinical Oncology*, 2 (1990), pp.79–83.

Review Articles

Royal College of General Practitioners, Clinical Information Folder on Terminal Care and Bereavement, *The Role of the Hospice* (1989)

Royal College of General Practitioners, Clinical Information Folder on Terminal Care and Bereavement, *The Psychological aspects of Terminal Illness* (1989)

Chapters in Books

'Bereavement' in *Death and Bereavement* ed. Austin H Kutscher, (Illinois, 1969).

'Communication between the Doctor and his Patients' in *The Practice of Family Medicine*, eds Coulter and Llewellyn, (Edinburgh, 1971).

'The Bereaved and their Hallucinations' in *Bereavement, its Psychological Aspects*, eds Schoenberg et al., (New York, 1975).

'Domiciliary Care of the Terminally Ill' in *Innovations in the Care of the Elderly*, eds Bernard Isaacs and Helen Evers, (Croom Helm Ltd., 1984).

'Terminal Care and Bereavement' in *Asian Health Care*, eds Brian R McAvoy and Liam Donaldson, (Oxford, 1989).

Books

Death and Bereavement: The psychological, religious and cultural interfaces. (London, 1997).

Healing in Perspective, (London, 2003).

Pointers to Eternity, (Talybont, 2010).

References

1   J Horder, *John Hunt*, a biographical memoir (London, 2002).

2   Ronald Rompkey (ed.), *The Labrador Memoir of Dr Harry Paddon* (Montreal, 2003), p.241.

3   Ibid., p.14.

4   Ibid., p.243.

5   Ibid., p.164–6.

6   Ibid., p.172.

7   Ibid., p.225.

8   R Ness, 'The impact of indigenous healing activity: an empirical study of two fundamentalist churches', *Social Science and Medicine*, 14B (1980), pp.167–80.

9   H Kaminer and P Lavie, 'Sleep and dreams in well-adjusted and less adjusted Holocaust survivors' in M S Stroebe, W Stroebe, R O Hanson (eds) *Handbook of Bereavement* (New York, 1993), pp.331–45.

10   J Berger, *A Fortunate Man. The Story of a Country Doctor* (London, 1967).

11   W D Rees, 'A Fortunate Man' in *An Anthology of Personal Views from the British Medical Journal* (London, 1971) pp.207–9.

12   W D Rees, 'Agricultural Tractor Accidents', *British Medical Journal*, 2 (1965), p.63.

13   P Fisher, *Hansard*, 864, 1973, pp.881–9.

14   W D Rees, 'The immediate care of road traffic and tractor accidents in a rural area', *Journal Royal College of General Practitioners*, 15 (1968), p.115.

15   W Gissane and J Bull, *The Practitioner*, 188 (1962), p.489.

16   W D Rees, 'Pregnant woman struck by lightning', *British Medical Journal*, 1 (1965), p.63.

17   J Morris, 'The Art of Talismanic Magic. Being selections from the works of Rabbi Solomon, Agrippa, Barrett etc.', 1888, NLW MS 11297C.

18   R Gibbings, *Coming Down the Wye*, (Boston, 1943), p.9.

19   Ibid., pp.129–30.

20   W D Rees, 'Physical and mental disabilities of 1,190 ordinary motorists', *British Medical Journal*, 4 (1967), p.593.

21 W D Rees and S Lutkins, 'Mortality of Bereavement', *British Medical Journal* 4 (1967), p.13.

22 W D Rees, 'The Hallucinations of Widowhood', *British Medical Journal*, 4 (1971), p.37.

23 W D Rees, 'The Distress of Dying', *British Medical Journal*, 3 (1972), p.105.

24 W D Rees, 'The opioid needs of terminal care patients', *Clinical Oncology*, 2 (1990), pp.79–83.

25 Rees, Low-Beer and Dover, 'Terminal cancer patients referred for hospice care, who were not terminally ill and did not have cancer', *British Medical Journal*, 295 (1987), p.318.

26 W N Pickles, 'Epidemic catarrhal jaundice. An outbreak in Yorkshire', *British Medical Journal*, 1 (1930), pp.944–6.

27 N Mathers, A Howe and S Field, 'Clinical research by GPs in their own practices', *British Journal of General Practice*, 59 (2009), pp.296–7.

28 J C Murdoch, 'The end of practice-based research?', *British Journal of General Practice*, 59 (2009), p.52.

29 D Seamark and C Seamark, 'Practice-based research', *British Journal of General Practice*, 59 (2009), p.691.

30 Seven original articles in *British Journal of General Practice*, 60 (2010), pp.721–69.

31 *British Journal of General Practice*, 60 (2010), Issues 570–81.

32 Joan Didion, *The Year of Magical Thinking* (London, 2005), pp.47–8.

33 Gerald O'Collins, *Easter Faith* (London, 2003), pp.12–13 and also 'The Resurrection and Bereavement Experiences', Irish Theological Quarterly, 76[3] (2011), pp.224–37.

34 Christine Valentine, *Bereavement Narratives* (London, 2008), p.183.

35 D Pereira Gray, 'Research general practices', *British Journal of General Practice*, 45 (1995), pp.516–17.

36 L F P Smith, (1997) 'Research general practices: what, who and why?', *British Journal of General Practice*, 47 (1997), pp.83–6.

Also from Y Lolfa:

Pointers
to Eternity
Dewi Rees

£12.95

Joshua Gerwyn Elias

A Doctor's Tale

y Lolfa

£7.95

General Practice as it was is just one of a
whole range of publications from Y Lolfa.
For a full list of books currently in print, send
now for your free copy of our new full-colour
catalogue. Or simply surf into our website

www.ylolfa.com

for secure on-line ordering.

TALYBONT CEREDIGION CYMRU SY24 5HE
e-mail ylolfa@ylolfa.com
website www.ylolfa.com
phone (01970) 832 304
fax 832 782